20TH-CENTURY COMPOSERS

A Polish Renaissance

A Polish Renaissance

by Bernard Jacobson

To my wife

Phaidon Press Limited
Regent's Wharf
All Saints Street
London N1 9PA

First published 1996
© 1996 Phaidon Press Limited

ISBN 0 7148 3251 0

A CIP catalogue record for this book is
available from the British Library

Printed in Singapore

Frontispiece, Bobo
Brinkmann and Uta-Maria
Flake as Adam and Eve in
the 1979 Stuttgart
production of Penderecki's
Paradise Lost, in the
background is Christ
(Raymond Wolansky).

Contents

Preface

When I started work on this book about four composers who have changed the shape of music in the second half of the twentieth century – Panufnik, Lutosławski, Penderecki, and Górecki – I thought I knew their music reasonably well. I admired all of them, though it is fair to say that I both knew and admired Panufnik the most. I had the privilege of his friendship for the last twelve years of his life, and the prospect of working with him was one of the main reasons I accepted a post at Boosey & Hawkes, his publishers, in 1979, staying there till 1984. With Lutosławski and Penderecki I had had much less personal contact, and I have never met Górecki, though the charm and force of character that emerge from his television persona are such that I feel I have, and talking to him on the telephone in recent months has enhanced the impression of genial warmth. But I knew they were all composers of stature.

What I expected might be the result when I went more deeply into their music was a reassessment of their respective importance. These things do happen. Maybe my estimate of Panufnik as the supreme master among twentieth-century Polish composers was due merely to closer acquaintance.

In the event, knowing the four much better now, I have come to admire all of them a great deal more, and to recognize the sheer size of their accomplishments, often achieved in appallingly difficult circumstances. I have learned to relish more keenly than ever the subtlety and allusive richness of Lutosławski's mind, and the range and boldness of Penderecki's invention. Górecki, whose work I had heard the least, has become an indispensable part of my musical world, by virtue of his contempt for sacred cows as much as for his revelations of true sanctity. And Panufnik is even better than I thought.

This book could not have been written without help from a number of people, to whom I am immeasurably grateful. The principal publishers of the four composers' work have responded promptly, enthusiastically, and with exemplary patience to repeated requests for information and for printed and recorded materials. My former colleagues and other newer staff members at Boosey & Hawkes have had to cope on more than one front, since they publish both Panufnik and Górecki: Janis Susskind and Susan Bamert have unfailingly pointed me in the right direction, and Emma Kerr and Nicole Rochman must have felt at times that the questions would never end, and yet went on ingeniously finding the answers. At Chester, the managing director himself, James Rushton, has put his knowledge of Lutosławski's music at my disposal without stint, backed up by his assistant Rebekah Young. At Schott's London office, Sally Groves and Ulrike Müller first gave me invaluable hints, and then directed me to the staff in Mainz, where Penderecki's music is actually published: there Bernhard Pfau, Regine Wolf, Klaus Rainer Schöll and Katja Riepl have overwhelmed me by the rapidity and thoroughness with which every last call for help has been answered.

You might say that all these people were just doing their jobs, but having been one of them in the past I know how hard it is to find the time to provide such services, and I am full of admiration. David Drew, also a former Boosey & Hawkes colleague, has answered a number of questions about Górecki; Adrian Thomas, who knows more about that composer than anyone else alive, has kindly allowed me to pick his brain; and Wolfram Schwinger has added further information to the wealth of it I had already gleaned from his excellent book about Penderecki. Then there is Beresford King-Smith, who went to enormous trouble to provide me with documentation of Panufnik's programmes during his two seasons as music director of the City of Birmingham Symphony Orchestra. John Schreurs, manager of the Albersen record shop in The Hague, has helped greatly in my search for discographical information. The distinguished biochemist Hilary Koprowski, who was a music student at the Warsaw Conservatoire at the same time as Panufnik and Lutosławski and also knows Penderecki well, has given me useful information. So has Professor Nicolaus Zwetnow, like Dr Koprowski a Renaissance man (including among his occupations neurosurgery, composing, playing the balalaika, and shooting a pistol in the Olympic Games for the team of his adopted country Norway), who got to know Lutosławski when the composer was staying at his summer home near Oslo. John Denison has answered with enviable clarity my questions about events in English music as far back as the 1950s, when he was Music Director of the Arts Council of Great Britain.

In a more general way, I owe a debt of gratitude to my old friend the English composer Wilfred Josephs for introducing me to Panufnik's music in the first place, back in the mid-1970s. There *are* composers able to feel and share such selfless enthusiasm for a colleague's work, but I wish they were more numerous. It was at Wilf's house, too, that I first met Lutosławski, even longer ago.

The idea of writing this book was proposed to me by Norman Lebrecht. To him, and (in order of appearance) to Suzanne Beadles, Roger Sears, Peter Owens, and Ingalo Thomson of Phaidon Press, my thanks are due for the delicacy, patience, understanding, and skill that they have brought to our collaboration.

Finally, there are two wives. Camilla Panufnik was indispensable, not only to her husband in smoothing his compositional path during the last thirty years of his life, but from 1979 onwards also to me in making every means of understanding his music readily available. In recent months (helped latterly by Susanna Smith, an admirable research assistant), she has devoted many hours to ferreting out facts and confirming or discounting my intuitions. And my wife Laura, in addition to serving as a reliable consultant on questions of diplomacy and cheerfully putting up with the domestic disruptions that go with writing a book, has also read the manuscript with an unerring eye for detail and pointed out numerous errors, some of which were quite funny.

If I have forgotten anyone, I apologize. None of those named should be held to account for the weaknesses of this book, but any strength it can lay claim to is largely due to them.

Bernard Jacobson
Den Haag, 1995

Prelude

There is no simple answer to the question of where contemporary Polish music came from. Entrenched in the soil that produced it is the ancient tradition of Polish folk music, along with a history of art-music composition that goes back more than four centuries. Another fostering element is the formidable intellectual tradition of Polish Roman Catholic thought.

Towards the middle of the twentieth century, the Nazi occupation obstructed access to any liberal tradition, whether of art or of philosophy, for all thinking Poles. Scarcely were the Germans gone when a new totalitarianism, this time imposed from Russia, placed limits that were in their different way even harsher on freedom of expression. For Polish composers at the end of our century and beyond, the demise of Communism – or perhaps (for who can say?) its revival – will have created yet another background.

So far as Penderecki and Górecki are concerned, Panufnik and Lutosławski themselves form part of the background, but in different ways. Lutosławski not only provided many Polish children in the 1940s and 50s with their first exposure to music in the shape of his folk-song arrangements: through the same children's student and adult years he was a national musical mentor in a more general sense. On the other hand, by the time Penderecki and Górecki reached their twenty-first birthdays, Panufnik had left Poland, and for the next two decades his music was almost totally unknown there.

To observers in the great established musical centres, horizons look very different from the way they appear at what may be called the periphery. It is true that in eighteenth-century Germany Georg Philipp Telemann, who had an inexhaustibly enquiring mind, was delighted by the rhythms and melodic turns of Polish folk music and introduced many of them to Western listeners. Long before that, moreover, the polonaise and the mazurka had both become popular throughout Europe. But until the four Polish composers under discussion began around 1960 to establish a commanding presence on

Folk music and Catholicism
are both central to Polish
life: *right,* bands play at the
Kazimierz festival; *below,* a
Highland dance in the Tatra
mountains

Above, kneeling pilgrims in Czestochowa's 600 - year-old church; *right,* participants in the annual Passion Play at Kalwaria Zebrzydowska

the international scene, music around the world was relatively little influenced by Polish art music. Even Chopin is not quite the gigantic exception he seems, for although much of what he brought to Paris came from the folk music of his native country, he drew much of the 'art' side of his music from French sources and from foreigners like Mozart, Beethoven, and Schubert.

Indeed, Polish music in general has found many sources of inspiration abroad, and not only in such times as the cultural thaw of the late 1950s, when access to the ferment of styles already prevalent in the West wrenched young Polish musicians out of their enforced isolation. Even Wacław z Szamotuł, one of the greatest Polish Renaissance masters, whose career reached its peak in the middle of the sixteenth century, was deeply influenced by the Dutch school of the day. In the court chapels where he was employed, the works of Lassus, Palestrina, Vittoria, and other foreigners were as central a part of the repertoire as anything written by their Polish contemporaries.

The pattern is repeated through history. Despite attempts at protectionism going back as far as the sixteenth century, pioneered by the guilds, which were the forerunners of today's musicians' unions, Italian influence in particular came to dominate many areas of Polish musical life in the Baroque period. From 1625 on, a stream of Polish students went to Rome to study with Girolamo Frescobaldi. Opera at the Polish courts remained obstinately Italian during the seventeenth and eighteenth centuries (which is hardly surprising if you consider that, in London, Covent Garden was still called the 'Royal Italian Opera', and still habitually performed Wagner, Meyerbeer, and Gounod in Italian, almost until the 1890s). In the early decades of the nineteenth century the Irish pianist-composer John Field, who lived much of his life in Russia and toured extensively around Europe, exerted a strong influence on Chopin through the conception and style of his nocturnes and concertos.

Chopin apart, the most important composers Poland produced through most of the nineteenth century were Stanisław Moniuszko, Henryk Wieniawski, and Ignacy Paderewski. Moniuszko's achievement was concentrated almost as narrowly in the operatic field as was Chopin's in that of piano music, and in any case Moniuszko was a figure of national rather than international importance. Wieniawski and Paderewski, though they wrote much charming

Dominant figures in
nineteenth-century Polish
music included, *right,*
Chopin, *far right,* the opera
composer Stanisław
Moniuszko, *below,* violin
virtuoso and composer
Henryk Wieniawski, and
below right, Ignacy
Paderewski, the
pianist–composer who
became Poland's first prime
minister in 1919.

music, were more strikingly gifted as performers than as composers. Thus, by the time a 'Young Poland' group constituted itself in 1906 around Grzegorz Fitelberg, Mieczysław Karłowicz, and the most talented composer of the generation, Karol Szymanowski, something of a creative vacuum had developed, and the group's agenda centred on filling that vacuum and on forcing Polish music to catch up with the last hundred years of Western European developments.

The real scope of Szymanowski's talent is not at issue here. Possibly if there had been less of a vacuum he would not have become so conspicuous a figure. His own stylistic explorations, reflecting the insecure foundations he had to build on, ranged through late Romanticism and neo-classicism to an eventual identification with his Polish folk-music roots, taking in a vivid interest in both the exotic and the erotic on the way.

Roughly halfway through Szymanowski's composing life, Panufnik and Lutosławski started theirs. By this time the labours of Szymanowski and his contemporaries were showing some results, and an intermediate generation was beginning to develop an international outlook and to attract international respect. Apart from Alexandre Tansman (who moved to Paris in his twenties) and Roman Palester (who left later, in the 1940s), Bolesław Woytowicz and Panufnik's teacher Kazimierz Sikorski were prominent members of this group, as were Artur Malawski and Bolesław Szabelski, who later taught Penderecki and Górecki respectively. But it was with the generation born between 1910 and 1915, which included Grażyna Bacewicz (and another emigrant, Michał Spisak) as well as Panufnik and Lutosławski, that mere respectability would be left behind.

In 1973, in a conversation with the Hungarian musicologist and publisher Bálint András Varga, Lutosławski paid emphatic tribute to Szymanowski's role:

He undertook a most difficult task: the transplanting of modern West European music onto Polish soil. His significance is immense, without him a whole generation of composers would be impossible to imagine.

Asked to explain the strength of the new development when it did come, Lutosławski spoke of the influence of Sikorski, Szabelski, and Woytowicz on their gifted pupils, but added:

Szymanowski, a devotee of both mystical poetry and life's pleasures, was the precursor of Poland's twentieth-century musical renaissance.

It is a coincidence that a number of interesting talents should have appeared in Poland at this particular historical moment. One reason probably is that the muse was silent for so long in our country. We do not have such a rich tradition as the Germans, Italians or the French. We are not yet surfeited, we are younger in music than other nations … our musical vein is not yet exhausted, we are fresh – and it is this freshness that unites Polish composers who have otherwise highly differing personalities.

One aspect of their differences is the variety of foreign influences to which the composers examined in these pages have responded. Lutosławski, on whose style the Polish folk heritage had the least profound effect, sounds in his fine artistic bones more French than anything else. This impression is supported by his claim to belong to the tradition of Debussy–early Stravinsky–Bartók–Varèse rather than to the Viennese line (though the closing pages of the Third Symphony recall Ravel, or even Respighi, more than Debussy). It is reinforced by the texts he chose for his vocal works, and borne out by the French aesthetic of one of his last large-scale works, *Chantefleurs et Chantefables,* completed in 1992. Next to all this refined sensibility, the elemental darkness and brooding psychological intensity of Penderecki evoke an unmistakably Austro-German effect; again, his choice of texts (when not setting Latin) and subjects, as well as his predominant sphere of activity, strengthens this impression.

Panufnik is something of a special case in this regard. He was part-English by descent, and lived nearly half his life in England. The influence of English poetry on his work is perhaps stronger than that of English music; yet there is also, in Panufnik's deep quietude, an affinity to be felt with Vaughan Williams, a composer he greatly admired, and there is no trace of the taste for expressionism we find in Penderecki. As an exile, Panufnik never lost his love of Polish folk music and art, nor his penchant for stringent organization of thought in the Polish intellectual tradition. The Polish folk strain blended happily with the English pastoral element in his later work, and the intellectual control kept both aspects from degenerating into self-indulgent nostalgic musing.

Górecki, like Penderecki, is a composer intent on the elemental, on the inner core of the universe and man's relationship with it. But in his case this concern produces more light than darkness. Some of that light may come by reflection from the transcendental musings of Messiaen, for him a supreme model. Nevertheless, there is little Frenchness in Górecki's music. Just as he has kept closer to his origins in residence and working environment than the other three, so his music has drawn more profoundly on the legacy of invention and feeling to be found there. Thus he may reasonably be called the most Polish of the four.

I

Panufnik rehearses
the London Symphony
Orchestra for a televised
performance of his *Sinfonia
di Sfere* at the 1977
Promenade Concerts in the
Royal Albert Hall, London.

*No other contemporary Polish composer can
replace Andrzej Panufnik as regards the
importance and the part he played in music,
and, even more, in the culture of the country
from which he came. Contrary to many of his
colleagues, his creativity retained some Polish
traits to the very end.*

Tadeusz Kacyński, in programme of
Park Lane Group concert, 18 October 1992

Andrzej Panufnik

In the ordinary way, a composer's biography tells itself best in the unfolding of his output, but sometimes *force majeure* intervenes. Biographically speaking, all of Mozart's works are early works, and so, for rather deeper musical reasons too, are all of Schubert's. By contrast, virtually all the works of Andrzej Panufnik are late works. In his case, this would not have been so but for the pressures of history.

Give or take a misstep or two, Panufnik's early years followed a path normal enough for the development of a creative musician. His father, Tomasz (born in 1876), had earned his living mostly as an engineer specializing in hydro-technology. But building violins was (as Andrzej put it in his autobiography, *Composing Myself*) his 'real passion', though the string-instrument factory he set up in 1921 folded through lack of capital.

In 1909, Tomasz married Matylda Thonnes, a 27-year-old violinist of partly English descent. The first of the couple's two children, Mirosław (Mirek for short), was born towards the end of that year, and Andrzej's birth, in Warsaw, followed on 24 September 1914.

Andrzej absorbed his early musical education largely by osmosis from his mother's playing. He started to compose when he was nine, soon after beginning piano lessons with his much-loved grandmother, and rapidly produced a 'sonatina' that was actually, he reports, 'just a simple melody in the right hand with a few chords in the left'. Owing to the social stigma still widely attached in 1930s Poland to the artistic professions, a performing career was never seriously envisaged for his mother. Nevertheless, though his father shared the view that music was not a profession for a gentleman, Andrzej was allowed at the age of eleven to enter the junior department of the Warsaw Conservatoire to continue his piano studies. But undermined both by discouraging teachers, and by the pressure of combining music with his regular *gimnazjum* (high school) homework, he succumbed to nerves in the end-of-year examination, and was debarred from attending further lessons on the ground that he had 'no musical talent'. The next four years sidetracked the fledgling composer. The examination failure confirmed his father's opposition to any more piano studies. Family financial problems forced Andrzej to move to inferior schools (though at one of them, through a friend whose passion was jazz, he was delighted to encounter Dixieland for the first time), and in 1929 he entered engineering school to train as an aircraft designer, another youthful enthusiasm.

Within a year, he found himself 'in a kind of spiritual and emotional vacuum … I had lost touch with music – and yet without music I myself was lost'. Fortunately, buoyed up by an invitation from the Warsaw education authorities to create and direct the first state school of instrument-making, Tomasz Panufnik yielded to his wife's urgings and agreed to Andrzej's studying music full-time, provided he return first to the municipal *gimnazjum* to matriculate.

By now too old to take the entrance examination for the Conservatoire piano department, and with too little formal training to try for the faculty of theory and composition, Andrzej worked on his own to catch up missed study-time. Much of his energy was devoted

Left, Panufnik's parents, Tomasz and Matylda, on their honeymoon in Samara, Siberia, in 1909; *above,* Andrzej, aged seven, with his twelve-year-old brother Mirek

to improvisation, sometimes in partnership with his brother's banjo, and to writing pieces influenced by Ellington and Gershwin. His recently discovered affinity with jazz styles paid off when, through the interest of an acquaintance of his mother's who owned a small music shop, a Panufnik foxtrot came to the notice of a well-known poet, Marian Hemar, who wrote a lyric for it. A popular comedian, Adolf Dymsza, performed the piece, *Ach Pardon*, in revue – triumphantly, though the composer, being under age for an adult show, was not allowed into the theatre to hear it. A successful gramophone record followed, as well as a request to write another foxtrot (*I Want No More*) for the same lyricist; young Panufnik found himself improbably well off, and was astonished to hear people whistling and singing his tune in the street.

Entrance to the Conservatoire still posed a problem for a student without formal qualifications, but Eugeniusz Morawski, the director of the Conservatoire, advised Panufnik to apply to the percussion department. He passed the relatively simple tests easily. And so finally, in February 1932, he re-entered the Conservatoire – part-time at first, since he still had to matriculate from the *gimnazjum* – as a percussion student with permission to sit in on theory, music history, and score-reading classes, and with the chance to resume serious piano studies. That same autumn, after matriculating, he became a full-time student at the Conservatoire, where he was allowed to switch immediately from percussion to theory and composition, and to join the student orchestra.

Panufnik at the age of seventeen, when he re-entered the Warsaw Conservatoire

Panufnik's musical education now accelerated sharply. He completed the theory and composition course in four years – the student with 'no musical talent' thus graduating in half the prescribed time. His early student works included a set of variations for piano and a *Classical Suite* that was performed publicly by a student string quartet. But it was the Piano Trio, written in the spring of 1934 when he was nineteen, that he was to describe in his autobiography as his first serious achievement in composition: 'If I had given my works opus numbers, I would have designated it as "Opus 1"'.

For his last academic year at the Conservatoire, 1935–6, Panufnik's teacher Kazimierz Sikorski gave him two composing assignments: a set of symphonic variations for orchestra, and then, as his diploma work, a large-scale piece for solo voices, chorus, and orchestra. From

Sikorski, Panufnik learned the unconventional method of setting a composition down on paper from the start as a full orchestral score (instead of beginning with a piano score and then orchestrating it), and this was to remain his practice throughout his career.

In general he found Sikorski 'dry, even discouraging'. Yet the professor's curt comment – 'bare, naked' – on the textural sparsity of two pieces Panufnik wrote during this time, Symphonic Allegro and Symphonic Image, was perhaps hardly an unwelcome assessment. As Panufnik remarks:

Obviously he would react against my pieces because, from my earliest years, I favoured clarity and economy of means of expression, making it my aim never to write a single superfluous note. Recognising that we differed in matters of taste, I settled to learn all the craftmanship I could from him, but determined meanwhile quietly to go my own way.

In any case, the psalm-setting that Panufnik offered as his graduation exercise won Sikorski's and the other professors' unanimous approval. Panufnik duly received the highest honour the Conservatoire could bestow on its graduates, a diploma with distinction. This brought the chance to conduct the Warsaw Philharmonic in a performance of his Symphonic Variations at the laureates' gala concert – he had attended some of Walerian Bierdiajeff's conducting classes – and the exhilaration of receiving his first-ever ovation from an audience.

Amongst the other performers in the graduation gala [Panufnik notes], my two close friends, both Witolds, were destined to become famous: Witold Małcużyński was playing the Liszt Piano Concerto and Witold Lutosławski, graduating as a pianist rather than a composer, played a concerto by Beethoven.

The years that followed his graduation in 1936 took Panufnik to Vienna, Paris, and London. Considering how to reach his goals, he decided that as a composer he had to find his own voice, and that the best way to learn more about music was by learning to conduct the classics. From the Foundation of National Culture he secured a grant to study for a year at the Vienna Academy. His intention to spend

Following page, a Warsaw street scene of 1939

Panufnik's service as an officer cadet was unwelcome but happily brief.

1936–7 there was deflected by a call-up for National Service, but his time as a soldier was mercifully cut short when he was released for medical reasons.

This happened in a prophetic way. Spending the night at his parents' home on the way to the medical examination, unable to sleep for worrying about his future, Panufnik turned on the radio:

Suddenly I heard music of unbelievable beauty: a simple line of melody sung in unison by women's voices. I had never heard it before and it seemed to transport me to another world. It was the first known Polish hymn, the Bogurodzica, a Gregorian chant dating from the Middle Ages.

Twenty-seven years later, that hymn was to form the basis of the *Sinfonia Sacra,* one of Panufnik's finest works and still probably his most popular symphony. For the moment, it mesmerized him. In a virtual trance, he drank innumerable cups of strong black coffee, and to his relief the accelerated heartbeat that resulted convinced the doctors at the Military Hospital that he was unfit for soldiering.

So Vienna was merely delayed for a year, during which Panufnik picked up valuable experience in Warsaw. Through family connections he was invited to write music for some radio plays. A brief stint as music critic for the radio served to show that this was a line of work he never wanted to tackle again. A film on which he collaborated as music editor, combining three Chopin studies with dance images, won a gold medal at the Venice Biennale. And one concert work, a *Little Overture,* was written at great speed and premièred by the Warsaw Philharmonic Orchestra. It was conducted by Grzegorz Fitelberg, formerly a fellow member with Szymanowski of the turn-of-the-century 'Young Poland' group of composers, but by this time dedicated to conducting and established as the leading champion of new Polish music.

Then it was time for Vienna. In a 1984 interview with Nigel Osborne for the journal *Tempo,* Panufnik explained why he chose Vienna, at a time when most of his fellow graduates were heading for Paris:

I had a chance of joining Weingartner's conducting class, and I had recently come across a score of Webern's Five Orchestral Pieces. I wanted to

*hear more of the music of the Second Viennese School, and also
entertained the hope of studying with Webern. In the event only half of
my plan worked out. I arrived in 1937. There was not a single
performance of Schoenberg, Webern, or Berg in the whole season …*

Felix Weingartner's class provided ample consolation. Weingartner
concentrated on teaching his students what Panufnik felt mattered
most in conducting technique: 'precision of movement at the tip of
the baton'. But it was for something beyond this – 'the ultimate
perception of what lies behind the notes, the ability to transmit
through the orchestra to the audience the true magic of the composer'
– that Panufnik admired Weingartner and Wilhelm Furtwängler
above all other conductors, and certainly above Toscanini, whom he
described years later as 'a great watchmaker'.

As for the Second Viennese School – the collective title commonly
given to Schoenberg and his pupils, most notably Webern and Berg –
he was reduced to reading their scores in the Academy library. Of the
three, he found Schoenberg the hardest nut to crack:

*Someone once perceptively observed that the notes in Mozart's music
love one another. I had the impression that Schoenberg's notes hated
each other.*

He felt closer to Webern's 'exquisite crystal-like structures', and
also responded warmly to the dramatic element in Berg. (Panufnik's
own explorations of the Schoenbergian serial technique – using the
twelve notes of the chromatic scale – will be considered in Chapter 3.)
But whether studying conducting or composing, Panufnik was not
destined to complete a full academic year of study in Vienna.
Growing social unrest, the collapse of the government, Austria's
annexation by Germany, the sight of Hitler riding through Vienna in
an open car, the spreading persecution of Jews: all this made Panufnik
increasingly uneasy, and a few days' respite on a steamer trip up the
Danube to Budapest (where he heard Kodály's Te Deum at the Liszt
Academy and met the composer) rendered Vienna all the more
depressing by contrast.

When Weingartner – not a Jew himself, but a dedicated anti-Nazi
– was replaced by an ideologically 'correct' teacher from Germany,

Felix Weingartner, one
of the leading conductors
of his time, rehearsing the
Vienna Symphony
Orchestra for a London
concert in 1936, the year
before Panufnik went to
Vienna to study with him

Panufnik decided to go back to Warsaw ahead of schedule. It was the
first of many occasions when politics was to distract him from the
essential business of his life. Weingartner, at a chance meeting in the
Academy corridor, urged him to stay long enough to get his diploma,
but Panufnik 'did not care to have a piece of paper stamped with the
Nazi swastika'. Instead, he asked for – and received – a personal
certificate confirming the work he had done, and a keepsake
photograph, which Weingartner inscribed to his 'talented pupil'.

Back in Warsaw, where he was frustrated by his compatriots'
ostrich-like refusal to confront the prospect of war seriously, Panufnik
planned the next stage of his education. Having studied the Viennese
classics at the feet of one of their greatest exponents, he wanted now
to immerse himself in twentieth-century music – to hear, not just
read, the works of Schoenberg, Berg, and Webern, as well as
Stravinsky, Bartók, and the modern French school spearheaded by Les
Six, the 'group of six'. He also wanted to get back to serious
composition on his own account. Financing the project by writing

a film score for his old associates of the Chopin project, he set off
in the autumn of 1938 to spend six months in Paris and then go on
to London.

At a Paris Opera performance of Debussy's *Prélude à L'Après-midi
d'un faune* danced by Serge Lifar, Panufnik was deeply impressed by
the conductor, Philippe Gaubert, who agreed to give him private
lessons in conducting French music (and who eventually refused to
accept any payment). From these studies, and from Paris's vibrant
concert life, Panufnik emerged with the conviction 'that Debussy was
the greatest poet among the composers of the early twentieth century'.
Stravinsky, Poulenc, Honegger, Milhaud, and the 'very promising'
young Igor Markevitch were also favourites. Most impressive of all was
Bartók's music, 'rich with rhythmical vitality, harmonic ingenuity and
a stunning feeling for tone colour'.

Despite the distractions of Paris, with its museums, its throng of
young musicians, and its irresistible restaurants, Panufnik settled
down to plan and write his first symphony. 'Before writing a single
note' – he recollects characteristically – 'I had to search for the
symphony's "architecture" and its musical material': this was to remain
the first priority with every work he wrote. Meanwhile, during a quiet
Christmas in Cannes, he made an orchestral version of Bach's D major
organ Prelude and Fugue.

With the first twenty pages of his symphony duly completed, he
set off in March 1939 for England. There he was to find the standards
of pre-war concert life high, but the conservative programmes hardly
stimulating for a questing mind. 'It was', Panufnik decided, 'a
moment in my life to look inward rather than outward', and he made
excellent progress on Symphony No. 1. He also discovered, in the
library of the British Museum, English composers of an earlier
century, such as Avison, Boyce, and Arne, who would figure on his
programmes with the City of Birmingham Symphony Orchestra
twenty years later. And if English concert life (and food) were
disappointing, Panufnik found much to admire in England's
architectural heritage, and in its people's politeness, respect for privacy,
and tolerance for political diversity and freedom of speech – qualities
that were to assume crucial importance for him after the experiences
of the next fifteen years.

Weingartner, in London to conduct at Covent Garden, urged

Panufnik to stay in England, and offered to help him establish himself as a conductor. But Panufnik was unable to ignore the calls of family and homeland. He went back to Warsaw, as planned, and, as it turned out, just before war engulfed his country.

In September 1939, Andrzej Panufnik, nearly twenty-five years old, was a composer with a solid professional training and (apart from film and radio music) a portfolio of nine or ten works, several of them successfully performed. He had studied conducting with a master of the art and won his approval, experienced life and music in three of the world's artistic capitals, and developed a capacity to overcome obstacles by determined work.

In a normal composing career, what would be expected over the next decade or two is a developing record of performances and a rapidly expanding output. If we look at Panufnik in 1961, more than twenty years later, we find a composer in his middle forties with (apart from some charming arrangements of old Polish music) a portfolio of about a dozen works. Then, in the last thirty years of his life, no fewer than thirty-six works appeared, half of them on a symphonic or concerto scale. With these he established himself belatedly as one of the major voices of music in our time.

What happened to most of those years of early maturity was essentially what happened to millions of people in central Europe in the middle and late twentieth century: first the Nazi occupation, then, with scarcely a breath of 'freedom' in between, the Soviet domination. Some creative figures did not survive the first of these, and many found their way through the second only at the cost of their artistic integrity. Panufnik did survive, and eventually he fulfilled his creative potential, but doing so took all his determination, as well as, in 1954, a decision of startling audacity.

When the war began, the Panufnik family was at least able to endure its privations together. To save money, Mirek, his wife, who was suffering from tuberculosis, and their three-year-old daughter moved back into the family home in Warsaw. For the next fifteen years, Panufnik would hardly ever have space or peace to concentrate on composing, and there were many other things to occupy him, such as volunteer work in the Anti-Aircraft Defence, soothing his parents' constantly worsening illnesses and insecurity, and simply searching for food.

To keep some sort of musical life going under the restriction of occupation, a number of cafés had started to feature well-known classical and light-music performers. Panufnik, a competent enough pianist, seized on the chance for communication and self-expression offered by this safety-valve. For a while he played with a violinist friend from the Conservatoire, Tadeusz Geisler. Then with Witold Lutosławski he set up a piano duo. Apart from specially composed pieces such as Lutosławski's Paganini Variations, they arranged and performed more than 200 works from all corners of the repertoire during the next three and a half years. Besides relatively official café performances, they also risked their lives by giving 'underground' concerts to raise funds for Resistance workers and Jewish artists in need. Of the pieces the two men wrote for these various purposes, apart again from the Paganini *jeu d'esprit*, all that remain are a few patriotic songs: Lutosławski's five *Pieśnie walki podziemnej* ('Songs of the Underground Struggle'), and Panufnik's *Four Underground Resistance Songs*, one of which, *Warszawskie dzieci* ('Warsaw Children'), seems to have attained virtually the status of an unofficial national anthem. These groups of songs have survived partly through widespread underground publication in Poland, and partly through the time-honoured method of oral transmission.

Before the winter of 1941 was over, despite all the distractions, Panufnik had succeeded in finishing Symphony No. 1, writing

The German army parades through Warsaw after its lightning conquest of Poland in 1939.

The streets of Warsaw saw a very different kind of life after the German invasion.

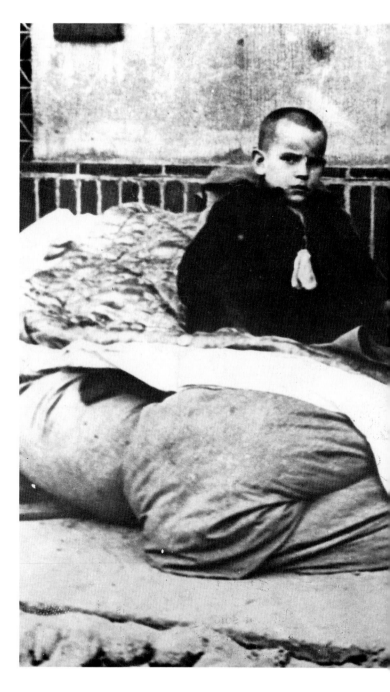

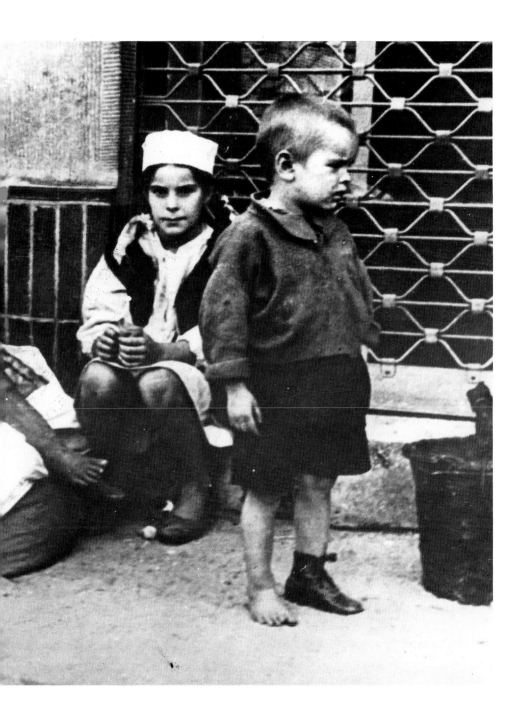

Symphony No. 2, sketching a *Heroic Overture* to celebrate the courage of the Polish defenders, and composing woodwind accompaniments for a set of Five Polish Peasant Songs. Partly to ease the overcrowding at home, he stayed for a while with a writer friend from his schooldays, Stanisław Dygat (whose sister Danuta later married Lutosławski). Then Panufnik's penchant for beautiful women asserted itself: he got to know Staszka Litewska, the widow of a cavalry colonel killed in action, and moved in with her and her two daughters. In those days, Poles could hardly plan a future, but there was the comfort of affection and companionship, and for Panufnik the additional benefit of a quiet room with a piano. It was here that, in 1942, he wrote his *Tragic Overture*, a significant step in the evolution of a new and personal musical language based on strictly limited thematic cells. He planned it as a purely abstract piece.

In order to scrape together a precarious wartime livelihood, Polish musicians without Nazi credentials were forced into the cafés and onto the streets.

In 1944, at a charity concert permitted by a slight relaxation of Occupation pressures, Panufnik conducted members of the Warsaw Philharmonic in the first performance of his *Tragic Overture*.

But when it was finished, he notes:

> *Though ostensibly I had kept to my rules, I realised that my intellectual disciplines had failed to control my unconscious, that the overture was interspersed with startlingly onomatopoeic passages – for example, the sound of a falling bomb (percussion); the soft engine noise of an aeroplane disappearing in the distance (trombones' glissando); a volley of machine guns (the burst of percussion in the final bars); the final chord shrieked out by the full orchestra, an agonising wail of despair.*

At this time family bereavements began to press on the Panufniks. Andrzej's cousin Antoni died in Auschwitz; his brother's wife, Maria, deprived of effective medicines, died of tuberculosis in 1943. Then a slight relaxation of the Germans' oppressive tactics enabled a Polish charity organization to plan fund-raising concerts, which Panufnik conducted after copying out all the orchestral parts by hand. At the first concert, in March 1944, surviving members of the Warsaw Philharmonic and their colleagues played Panufnik's 1938 Bach orchestration, his *Tragic Overture*, and Mozart's D minor Piano Concerto. The second programme, two months later, included Panufnik's Second Symphony. After its première Panufnik heard jubilant shouts – 'We have a conductor for the Warsaw Philharmonic when the war is over!' – but what must have meant more to him was his father's praise: 'It was the first occasion that he rescinded his overt disapproval of my chosen profession'.

The easing of the pressures of the Occupation was short-lived. Renewed tensions in Warsaw, and his mother's failing health, led Panufnik to move her out of the city to a small villa with a garden in the suburbs where he had managed to rent rooms; his father, inseparable from his violin collection, stayed at home. Andrzej went to look after her, and left all his music at Staszka's flat. But before he could return, the Soviets' advance set the stage for what would be a cataclysm both for Warsaw and for Panufnik himself. On 1 August 1944, encouraged by Russian broadcasts promising military support, the citizens began their Uprising. Within two months, cynically left to their own devices by the Soviet army, they suffered losses of a quarter of a million killed by the Nazis, and a defenceless and devastated city was ripe for 'liberation'.

Tomasz Panufnik escaped, injured but alive, to rejoin his wife. Mirek, a dedicated resistance worker to the last, was killed, and his orphaned daughter Ewa came to live with Andrzej and his parents. The Soviet take-over was complete by March 1945. Staszka was alive, but had settled elsewhere. So Panufnik had two primary missions. He returned to the city, found his brother's body, and took it to the family tomb in the Powacki Cemetery. Then he went to Staszka's flat, improbably still standing among the ruins, in apprehensive search of the manuscripts that represented twelve years of compositional work.

His apprehension was justified. The woman who had taken over the flat had thrown every page away.

Suddenly, Panufnik found himself a thirty-year-old composer with not a single work to his name. What was needed for his own career, as for Polish musical life, was reconstruction. For both, this began in Kraków, which now temporarily resumed its old central role as the cultural capital of Poland.

Opposite, the statue of Christ the Redeemer in Warsaw's Three Cross Square, seen against the background of devastation in the aftermath of the 1944 Uprising.

Panufnik was first pressed into service as composer and music director of the Polish Army Film Unit, later known as Polish State Film Productions. It was based in Lódź, which was close enough to Kraków for him to develop his contacts with cultural life there. The Film Unit was to remain his main source of income as long as he stayed in Poland. Much of the work was distasteful: tightening Soviet political control ensured a high proportion of such films as *The*

Wawel od strony Wisły   Kraków —

With Warsaw in ruins, the ancient city of Kraków temporarily resumed its former role as Poland's cultural capital.

Electrification of the Villages, but there were also opportunities to work on documentaries illustrating artistic treasures like the Renaissance altarpiece in St Mary's Church in Kraków.

Alongside his duties at the Film Unit, Panufnik was soon swept up in the process of rebuilding Poland's orchestras. Seen at that time as the country's leading composer, he was also the logical successor to the conductor Fitelberg (who did not return from his wartime activities in western Europe and America till 1947). Offered the conductorship of the Kraków Philharmonic Orchestra, Panufnik almost turned it down because of his Film Unit commitments and the urgent need to start serious composing again. But the temptation of working with the country's best orchestra – and the right it would give him to family accommodation in Kraków (though his mother died soon after moving there) – proved irresistible. Thus a pattern evolved that was to persist for years: any idea of building, or even merely rebuilding, his musical output was relegated to the background by the necessities of everyday life.

Nevertheless, unable to get the *Tragic Overture* out of his mind, Panufnik decided to reconstruct it from memory. The taut, schematic structure of the piece made this task easier than he expected, and he went on to do the same with the Five Polish Peasant Songs and the even earlier Piano Trio. He also tackled Symphony No. 1, and received excellent reviews when he performed it in November 1945. In a typical press comment, it was greeted as 'a lyrical, sincere, and inspired work, very melodious, and interesting in construction'. But this time he was dissatisfied with the musical result: he destroyed the score himself, and decided to devote his future efforts instead to newly composed work. This in turn became a remoter prospect when a piano-teacher cousin who had lost her home in the Uprising was compassionately taken into the Panufniks' flat, where the din of her 'untalented beginners … battering the out-of-tune piano in the next room' made composing impossible again.

Meanwhile the pattern of official distractions intensified. Tadeusz Ochlewski, head of the new state music publishing house in Kraków (PWM, or Polskie Wydawnictwo Muzyczne), asked Panufnik to help in getting the enterprise under way. And his success with the Kraków Philharmonic was such that, at the end of just one season, he was appointed music director of the Warsaw Philharmonic.

Again, there was a complete orchestral organization to be rebuilt from scratch. Performing materials were impossible to obtain in Poland, and Panufnik was granted a passport to go and buy them in Paris. There he met the celebrated composition teacher Nadia Boulanger, and – at a private recital in the luxurious home of the Princesse de Polignac – Yehudi Menuhin. Before going home he gave some broadcast talks about Polish music for the French radio, and met its music director, the composer Henry Barraud, who invited him back to conduct the Orchestre National the following August.

For this engagement, in addition to music by Bach and Mozart and his own *Tragic Overture*, he programmed works by Michał Spisak and Antoni Szałowski, two Poles living in Paris, thereby getting into trouble on his return home for supporting colleagues who had turned their backs on Poland. But though his independence of mind occasionally infuriated the authorities, Panufnik was by now established internationally as the chief figure in contemporary Polish music. In that capacity he was, as he puts it, 'frequently shunted abroad by the Ministry of Culture' as a useful propaganda exhibit of national musical rebirth. Another prized invitation took him to the International Society for Contemporary Music's festival in London. There he gave a performance of his Five Polish Peasant Songs, and seized the opportunity of catching up with what was happening on the world composing scene.

A 1946 document identifies Panufnik as Director of the Warsaw Philharmonic; eight years later his tenure was deleted from the orchestra's records when he 'ceased to exist' after escaping to the West.

By 1947, on the other hand, the Warsaw Philharmonic situation was turning into a quagmire of political and bureaucratic obstructionism. First the Palladium Cinema, originally promised to the orchestra as a makeshift but adequate concert hall, suddenly became unavailable. Then, when the authorities reneged on their promise of living accommodation for musicians coming to the capital to join the orchestra, Panufnik resigned his post.

Now at last he would have the chance to write his first new music (apart from film scores) since the *Tragic Overture* of five years earlier. Very few composers can have had to endure so long a period of enforced silence as Panufnik's between the ages of twenty-seven and thirty-two. But he found to his relief that the creative machinery was still in working order, and in 1947 produced three important new works. Not only did they double his extant output: they also extended the technical and stylistic advances of the *Tragic Overture* in ways later seen as the very spearhead of the innovations of 'the Polish School'.

Using his fluency at the piano as an initial springboard back to composition, Panufnik first wrote a substantial solo work, *Circle of Fifths,* later retitled *Twelve Miniature Studies.* Next came the orchestral *Nocturne,* essentially composed during night-time strolls through the streets of Kraków (since the cousin's pupils still precluded composing in the family flat) and written down afterwards. A break for conducting engagements took Panufnik to Copenhagen for the next ISCM festival and on to England for an all-Beethoven programme – on one rehearsal – with the London Philharmonic in Brighton.

A brief stop in London produced the year's third new composition. Another fruit of Panufnik's nocturnal walking habit, it was conceived as he gazed down at the Thames from Waterloo Bridge – shades of Wordsworth's ode, similarly inspired 150 years earlier just two bridges up-river at Westminster. *Lullaby,* a delicately shimmering reverie for twenty-nine solo strings and two harps, was sketched in London and completed in full score when the composer returned to Poland. A final, smaller product of this fertile year was a string-orchestra arrangement of trio movements by the eighteenth-century Polish composer Felix Janiewicz, titled Divertimento.

A series of concerts in Berlin (with the famous Philharmonic), Leipzig, and Dresden followed. Despite an attack of pneumonia, Panufnik's conducting was a triumphant success, and he was urged on

A programme cover from 1948 illustrates Panufnik's distinguished career as a guest conductor.

BERLINER PHILHARMONISCHES ORCHESTER

all sides to stay in Germany and pursue his career there. But apart from his rewarding role in Polish musical regeneration (and his responsibility to his father), there was another deterrent factor:

Though I had steadfastly refused to join the Communist Party, I was not enamoured of the Western powers either; my resentment was deepened by the realisation that Roosevelt had sold my country to Stalin at the Yalta Conference of 1945 … Poland to my mind was still a separate nation, and I was determined to stay loyal to our government even if I regretted its need to bend before political pressures.

In 1948 Panufnik wrote his biggest postwar piece so far, his first surviving symphony. He called it *Sinfonia Rustica*, choosing a title rather than a number out of sentimental regard for his two lost works in the genre. A product of his affection for the folk music of northern Poland, it was the first of many works in which he based his musical structure on a visual analogy, in this case the colourful and symmetrical peasant paper-cuts of the region.

Sinfonia Rustica was to play a pivotal role in Panufnik's relations with the Polish state. First performed in Kraków in 1949, it won the Chopin Competition; in February 1950 Panufnik was sent to Budapest to record it for the Hungarian radio. Yet, in that same year, at a meeting of the Composers' Union, the man who had served as chairman of the Chopin Competition jury stigmatized the work as 'alien to the Socialist era', and Włodzimierz Sokorski, Deputy Minister of Culture and Art, declared, *'Sinfonia Rustica* has ceased to exist!'

What lay behind this volte-face was the long arm of Stalin's cultural commissar Andrey Zhdanov. In February 1948, he had launched an attack on a number of leading Soviet composers for the alleged 'formalistic perversions and anti-democratic tendencies in music … the cult of atonality, dissonance, and discord … infatuation with confused, neurotic combinations that transform music into cacophony'. For Shostakovich and his compatriots, it was 1936 all over again. Now the Soviet ideology gradually extended its grip also over art in the satellite nations, and under Sokorski's direction, abetted by the dedicated Marxism of the musicologist Zofia Lissa, the doctrine of 'socialist realism' was imposed on Polish composers as the basis of all valid musical creation.

It is curious that a work as genially tuneful – and folk-oriented – as *Sinfonia Rustica* should have become a casualty of this policy, but that is the kind of thing that happens when politicians take power over art. The next four years saw Panufnik treated to what he calls 'a stick-and-carrot technique'. On account of its unsatisfactory ideological character, his music was increasingly withheld from Polish audiences (though performances abroad were encouraged for their propaganda value). Meanwhile awards were showered on him. In 1949 he had received the Standard of Labour, First Class, which brought various privileges, including the assignment of a small flat in Warsaw to which he was able to move with his father. In 1951, and again in 1952, he was State Laureate of Poland.

Simultaneously, administrative and propaganda demands on his time were again making life and composition harder. Already pressured into accepting the vice-presidency of the Composers' Union, he was forced into active participation in the Committee for the Defence of Peace, sent off to the USSR 'to study Soviet teaching methods' in 1950, and dispatched to one window-dressing congress after another. They had, of course, to be of the right political complexion: Panufnik's election as Vice-President of the Music

Andrey Zhdanov, Communist Party Chief for the Leningrad Area, spearheaded the Soviet doctrine of 'socialist realism' in the arts during the 1930s and 40s.

Council of UNESCO (jointly with Arthur Honegger) was officially welcomed as a national honour – but he was never allowed to go to Paris for the Council's meetings.

Nor was Panufnik's personal life helping. The next in the series of beautiful women had appeared on the scene. In her early twenties, Marie Elizabeth O'Mahoney, born in London of Irish parentage, was known to all her friends as Scarlett 'because of her resemblance, both in character and physique, to the heroine of the film, *Gone with the Wind*'. When she met Panufnik she was on her honeymoon with her third husband, having arrived in Poland to live with her first only four years earlier. Panufnik commented laconically on their first encounter: 'My reaction was instant – I lost my head'. It does not take much perception, reading between the lines and looking at the relationship as it developed later, to see their marriage on 13 July 1951 as that of an

Panufnik with his first wife Scarlett, pictured in London after his 1954 escape from Poland by way of Zurich

impressionable man captivated by a volatile young woman whose
vulnerability appealed as compellingly to his chivalrous nature as her
beauty triggered his susceptibility.

The small flat Panufnik shared with his sick father was already
crowded: the housekeeper who doubled as his father's nurse had to
sleep in the kitchen. Two months after Andrzej's marriage, his father
died. Then Scarlett became pregnant, and a daughter, Oonagh, was
born in September 1952.

On the creative front, apart from the choral and orchestral
Symphony of Peace that Panufnik was manoeuvred into writing, the
production of these years was understandably meagre: in 1949 a set of
vocalises on folk melodies later published as *Hommage à Chopin*, and
in 1950 and 1951 two more essays in the recomposition of earlier Polish
music (*Old Polish Suite* and *Concerto in modo antico*), which afforded
'a pleasurable and absorbing way of escaping suffocation from political
pressure'. Then, in 1952, Panufnik returned to the idea of the *Heroic
Overture* conceived under the Nazi threat thirteen years before:

> *This time the nature of our invasion was more psychological than
> physical, but the need to assert defiance and faith in our future was
> greater than ever.*

Forthright and exultant in tone, the piece won first prize in a pre-
Olympic competition, and Panufnik conducted it in Helsinki at the
1952 Olympic Games. Characteristically, the Polish establishment saw
it as material for export only: after a try-out in Katowice, the *Heroic
Overture* was condemned as 'formalistic' and 'decadent', and duly
banned from further performance in Poland.

The next two years brought all the mounting personal and
political pressures to a head. In 1953, while heading a cultural mission
to China, Panufnik heard the news that his eight-month-old daughter
had drowned: Scarlett, who suffered from epilepsy, had lost
consciousness while bathing her. He was permitted to return to
Warsaw only after conducting the gala concert to be given that
evening in the presence of Chairman Mao. The additional strain their
baby's death put on the relationship of an obsessively private
composer and a wife with a powerful need for social activity can
readily be imagined.

In Beijing as head of a 1953 Polish Cultural Delegation, Panufnik speaks before conducting a concert in the presence of Mao Tse-tung.

In the aftermath of Stalin's death in the same year, Polish composers expected a relaxation in the political control over their work. At a crucial session of the Council of Culture and the Arts in the spring of 1954, however, Minister Sokorski dashed their hopes with a hard-line speech reaffirming the commitment to 'socialist realism' in art.

For Panufnik, the final straw came soon after. Comrade Ostap-Dłuski, an official in the foreign affairs department of the Communist Party, asked him to write 'personal' letters to his Western colleagues, urging their support for the Polish 'Peace Movement'. Behind this request – actually a directive – Panufnik saw the authorities planning to exploit his international prestige as a means of gathering information on musicians abroad, 'to find out whose sympathies or vanities might best be exploited, just as in the past they had exploited Picasso, Eluard, Sartre and many others'.

The only solution, he decided, was to leave Poland. And when he went, he hoped 'to make enough clatter to ensure that the whole world would hear about the Hell experienced by creative artists in the countries of the Eastern bloc'. It would be a leap into an unknown future. He had no idea whether he would be able to make a career abroad. But he could not do his work as a composer at home anyway. Apart from the factitious *Symphony of Peace*, an accomplished if modestly scaled wind quintet written in 1953 (which resurfaced in Poland in 1994), and the pieces based on old Polish music, the last five or six years had produced just one new work, and that was a seven-minute overture.

At first uncomprehending, Scarlett came to see that he was in an impasse. She agreed to help plan his escape. The idea they devised was for her to get out of the country first, securing permission on the coincidental ground that her father was seriously ill in London. Once safely in England (the obvious choice not only because of Scarlett's connections there but because of Andrzej's maternal ancestry), she would seek help from Panufnik's expatriate friends in organizing a conducting invitation for him in the West.

Scarlett later recounted the whole saga, worthy of the pages of Frederick Forsyth or John le Carré, in a melodramatic book published under the title *Out of the City of Fear*. Konstanty Regamey, Swiss-Russian by birth, and a former fellow student of Panufnik's at the Warsaw Conservatoire, who now lived in Zurich, proved to be the key figure in the plot: he enlisted the support of the Swiss composer Rolf Liebermann, who was director of music at the Zurich Radio.

Panufnik was duly summoned to the offices of the Committee for Cultural Relations Abroad and told to pack his bags: he had been invited to record a programme of contemporary Polish music with the Zurich Radio Symphony Orchestra, and the date, 7 or 8 July, was just two weeks away. Forcing himself to dissemble – for eagerness might have aroused suspicion – Panufnik asked if they couldn't send someone else – he was far too busy writing a new work.

This had the desired effect, and the official insisted. One small case was enough to hold both the conductor's uniform and the composer's exiguous output of scores. With it he left Warsaw, which he would not see again for thirty-six years. After various alarms in Zurich, and amid the clearly increasing suspicions of the Polish Legation there, he safely boarded a plane for London. Scarlett had already been in contact with the British Foreign Office. On the morning of 14 July 1954, she met him at Heathrow, together with two Special Branch representatives who conducted the couple to a secret refuge somewhere on the upper Thames.

The notion that economic forces press on mankind as harshly as any kind of political oppression, however partial and inaccurate as a formulation of Marxist thought, is nevertheless a version of it to which even non-Marxists have attributed some validity. Within a short time of his receiving asylum in England, Panufnik himself must have started to reflect on it rather ruefully. Had he gained political emancipation at the cost of financial ruin?

There was a brief flurry of excitement at his defection. His declaration, 'I hope very much that my protest will help my fellow composers still living in Poland with their struggle towards liberation from the rigid political control imposed upon them,' was widely reported in the West. But his public statements embarrassed the reasonable-minded liberals who were leaning over backwards to give the benefit of every possible doubt to the Communist regimes. Despite Britain's vaunted freedom of speech, Panufnik was asked to delete passages from articles he wrote for *The Times* on the ground that they were 'too anti-Communist'. Predictably, the Polish government reacted to his flight by confiscating all his possessions,

Leopold Stokowski, here shown at the piano in discussion with the English composer Ralph Vaughan Williams, was the first great conductor to champion Panufnik's music.

including his father's collection of instruments; performances of his
music, and even the mention of his name in future publications,
were banned.

The rebuilding of Panufnik's career was likewise a patchy business.
Initial financial help came from some British composers, notably
Ralph Vaughan Williams and Arthur Benjamin. Another supporter
was the former singer Sir Steuart Wilson, at this time Deputy General
Administrator of the Royal Opera House, who put Panufnik in touch
with the Harold Holt agency. The resulting concert with the
Philharmonia Orchestra at the Royal Festival Hall on 4 October
ended with Panufnik's *Nocturne*. It was greeted with a standing
ovation and some highly favourable reviews; but Panufnik's net
financial profit from this conducting engagement was £6 10s – the rest
of the fifty-guinea fee had gone to defray the cost of the extra players
needed to play the *Nocturne*. Other engagements that year included a
series of concerts with the Belgian National Orchestra in Ghent and
Brussels, with Joseph Szigeti as soloist in the violin concertos by
Mendelssohn and the great Swiss-born, Dutch-domiciled composer
Frank Martin.

In February 1955 Panufnik went to the United States for a Detroit
performance of his choral and orchestral *Symphony of Peace* conducted
by Leopold Stokowski, who had already performed the *Tragic
Overture* with the New York Philharmonic and now became one of
Panufnik's most dedicated champions. The performance, however,
confronted the composer with all the weaknesses of a score 'written in
a hurry and under duress from the Polish authorities', and in spite of
Stokowski's protests he subsequently withdrew the work. By the end
of the following year, he had recast it as a purely orchestral symphony
in one movement, titled *Sinfonia Elegiaca* and dedicated to the victims
of World War II; it was Stokowski again who gave the première, this
time in Houston, Texas, in January 1957. Other positive portents
included a July 1955 engagement to conduct *Sinfonia Rustica* at a
Promenade Concert with the BBC Symphony Orchestra, and a
contract with Boosey & Hawkes Music Publishers, who took over all
Panufnik's existing works from PWM – with the revisions necessitated
by such a transaction – and were henceforth to be his only publishers.

By this time, through the intercession of his old friend Witold
Małcużyński, Panufnik had received a substantial cheque from a

Polish-born Argentinian, Madame Rosa Berenbau, 'to help him start
to compose again'. He promised to dedicate his next major work –
which in the circumstances should have been a piano concerto for
Małcużyński – to this generous patron of the arts. He could hardly
have guessed at the time how long it would be before that piece could
be written. Thoughts of the piano concerto had first to be put aside
when the BBC commissioned a piece to celebrate the tenth
anniversary of the Third Programme. *Rhapsody* was completed in 1956.
Though not of symphonic scope, it is a thoroughly attractive piece,
showcasing the various members of the orchestra, and like Alberto
Ginastera's *Variaciones concertantes* well suited to serve programmers of
children's concerts as an occasional alternative to Britten's familiar
Young Person's Guide.

By 1956 Panufnik's marriage, which seems never to have been a
marriage of minds, was falling apart: he saw Scarlett as a person
'driven by a craving for excitement and glamour; a lifestyle with one
social adventure following another', while all he wanted was the peace
and solitude to compose. The surroundings of the small flat the
couple had taken in South Kensington had proved unexpectedly
noisy. Apart from all this, Panufnik had quickly realized that
conducting would have to be the first source of income to set him up
in England and that any large-scale composing projects would have
to wait.

Despite its meagre financial results, that Philharmonia Orchestra
concert in 1954 had been much talked about in English musical
circles, both for the impact made by the *Nocturne* and for the quality
of the conducting. John Denison of the Arts Council of Great Britain
had become an enthusiastic admirer. He now introduced Panufnik to
the directors of the City of Birmingham Symphony Orchestra, who
were looking for a successor to Rudolf Schwarz. After a successful trial
concert, Panufnik was offered the post of music director, and with it
the prospect of a solution to his financial problems. But accepting
would also make composing time scarcer than ever, what with the
demands of preparing fifty concerts a year, many of them on the road,
and the administrative and social commitments of such a post.

Asked to sign a three-year contract, Panufnik negotiated instead
for two years with an option to renew. He moved to Birmingham as
the contract required – thus completing the break with Scarlett, who

Panufnik conducting the European première of his Tenth Symphony, at the opening concert of the 1990 Warsaw Autumn Festival; this performance marked his return to Poland after thirty-six years of politically enforced absence.

was not prepared to share his provincial 'exile' – and inaugurated his tenure there on 12 September 1957 with a programme that began as he intended to continue. The evening opened with a concerto by Charles Avison, one of the eighteenth-century English composers he had discovered on his first visit to London in 1939, and closed with a graceful bow to both England and Poland in the shape of Elgar's *Polonia*. In the thirty-six different programmes Panufnik conducted in Birmingham over the next two years, some nineteen works of British composition were featured, and a further twenty appeared in the programmes of his guest conductors. Besides this, a series of Bach-Beethoven-Brahms evenings during the 1958–9 season enabled him to put into practice some of the classical principles he had imbibed from Weingartner's training and Furtwängler's concerts.

The first Birmingham season was bedevilled by artistic differences with the orchestra's leader, Norris Stanley, a difficult man whom many regarded as a mediocre musician. Panufnik eventually insisted on his dismissal, warning the Management Committee that he would not be able to continue as conductor otherwise, and with the Australian Wilfred Lehmann, who replaced Stanley, he was able to work happily enough in his second season. Pleased with the overall success of the collaboration between conductor and orchestra, the management asked Panufnik to stay. But he had managed to write only one new piece since his move to Birmingham: a *Polonia* of his own, suggested by Elgar's but quite different in its folklorish atmosphere, which he composed in London between the two Birmingham seasons. Desperate for time to compose, and feeling financially better off after saving most of his two years' salary, he regretfully refused, and moved back to London.

It did not take him long to realize that his resignation was a badly-timed move in terms of musical politics. The retirement of his supporter Richard Howgill as the BBC's Controller of Music had brought a successor. William Glock, Controller of Music at the BBC from 1959 to 1973, was to drag British musicians and audiences into the forefront of twentieth-century musical creativity – but with a stylistic tendency that would, ironically, pose serious problems for Panufnik himself. Glock's programming gave enormous emphasis to the Schoenberg school and its avant-garde descendants. Individualists like Panufnik and many of his British counterparts, on the other hand, were crowded out by the new quasi-totalitarian policy, and many of their works were designated 'unsuitable for broadcast on any wave-length'. A decade earlier, in Poland, Panufnik had been too modern: now, in the democratic West, he suddenly found himself in effect banned as too traditional.

Soon after leaving Birmingham, he met Winsome Ward, a member of the British Council's visual arts staff, with whom he was soon involved in a warm and loving if very brief relationship. But Panufnik, now nearly forty-five, was determined not to marry again: if ever composing was to come first for him, it must be now.

He had to do something to counter both the personal pressures and the stagnation of his career. Breaking off the relationship with Winsome, he sold the remaining two years of the lease on his South Kensington flat (which Scarlett, on the way to a fifth marriage, had already left), and went to the United States to see whether his future might be more promising on that side of the Atlantic. The trip yielded nothing in the way of conducting engagements despite Stokowski's energetic help. But while he was there Panufnik approached the Kosciuszko Foundation with the idea of writing a work to celebrate Poland's 1966 celebration of 1,000 years of statehood. It would be titled *Sinfonia Sacra*, and in tribute to Poland's rich cultural and Catholic tradition it would incorporate the melody of the *Bogurodzica* hymn that had struck his imagination so forcibly in 1936. Supported by the foundation's president, Professor Stephen Mizwa, Panufnik succeeded in securing a commission.

If anything, this further complicated the situation he faced on returning to England. His conducting income had dried up. Having already (through the help of Stephen Lloyd, chairman of the CBSO Management Committee) been offered a Feeney Trust commission to complete the piano concerto sketched a few years earlier, he now had two major works to write. Yet he was also busy with a chamber-orchestra piece, *Autumn Music*, begun amid the peaceful optimism of 1959, soon after his meeting with Winsome Ward. He had already been receiving reproachful letters from her; now he learned that she was terminally ill with cancer.

Work on *Autumn Music*, interrupted by conducting engagements in London and Buenos Aires and by the American expedition, obsessed him again. Dedicated to the memory of Winsome Ward, who died at the beginning of 1962, *Autumn Music* had taken on a radically different character. The opening idyll, returning after a doom-laden central section dominated by the inexorable tolling of a single note in the piano's lowest register, sounds idyllic no longer, but reverberates with the bitterly ironic awareness of lives passing and seasons revolving against the background of nature's unchanging indifference.

Though Panufnik, emotionally drained by his visits to Winsome in hospital, did not know it at the time, the influence that was to change everything had already appeared in his life. Just before his American trip in 1960, Camilla Jessel had come to see him. In her early twenties, the daughter of a retired naval commander, she had worked her way around the United States in a variety of secretarial jobs. Back in England, she became personal assistant to Neil Marten, who had looked after the Foreign Office arrangements for Panufnik's defection and was now a Conservative candidate in the general election. Marten felt that Camilla's combination of administrative skills and love for music could be useful in helping an unpractical composer to organize his life. Panufnik was immediately impressed by her capacity to listen, and by her qualities of stillness and understanding.

At that time he had been on the point of leaving for the States, and she for Paris to study French literature at the Sorbonne for a year, so any collaboration was moot, and they might not even have met again. When he had returned to England at the end of 1960, the Martens found him a room to rent in the Oxfordshire village of Adderbury: Camilla's parents lived in the same village, but this, too, he did not know till two years later, and in any case Camilla herself was still away at the Sorbonne.

Early in 1961, having finished *Autumn Music*, Panufnik embarked on the task of completing his piano concerto for its première the following January. A gentle enquiry from the States about progress on the Kosciuszko commission prompted him to make a few sketches for *Sinfonia Sacra*, but the chief effort had to be on the concerto. When it was finished, Panufnik left his cramped room in Adderbury for a rented country cottage near the Surrey village of Dockenfield, where the first priority was the completion of *Sinfonia Sacra*.

In December, needing a suitable signature on the documents for his British passport application, Panufnik arranged to get it from Neil Marten, who was now a Member of Parliament. When he arrived at the House of Commons, Camilla, now back from Paris, and establishing herself as a professional photographer, was there too. They had tea together, and at Marten's suggestion went on to set up a plan for the kind of secretarial help he had originally thought of the previous year.

As Camilla Panufnik remembers it now, Andrzej's life was going badly in 1960. He was facing the personal emptiness that would result from the inevitable break with Winsome; and, close to despair about his professional future, he was ready to contemplate leaving England, of which he had had such high hopes, for good if the United States offered better possibilities. In January 1962, after the première of the Piano Concerto (with Kendall Taylor as soloist, since Małcużyński had been too busy to study the work), a new pattern emerged: *Sinfonia Sacra* was progressing well (though Panufnik took a little time off writing it to compose a short string-orchestra piece called *Landscape*); and Camilla was driving down to Dockenfield regularly for an afternoon sorting out his correspondence and following up promising prospects. Also, the two fell in love.

As a distinguished professional photographer, Panufnik's second wife, Camilla Jessel, made a prolific pictorial record of his last three decades.

The courtship took nearly two years. In the summer of 1962, shunning too deep an involvement when he knew that he was 'never, never, never going to get married again', he tried to stop seeing her, but the attraction was too strong. Then, wanting urgently to finish the symphony and unwilling to face another English winter in his Spartan cottage, he went off to southern Spain: there, at Calpe, the score was finished during the next few months at a deserted hotel with a piano. But his strength of will had its limits: at his urging, Camilla, who had countered his move by arranging to go on a photographic mission for Save the Children in East Africa in January, first came for a visit over Christmas and the New Year, and then on her way back to London spent some days with him in Madrid and Paris.

Faced with Camilla's masterly non-pressure, Panufnik was beginning to realize that he was going to propose marriage in spite of all his misgivings. But as a traditional Polish gentleman of high principles, he could not do so when he had no financial security to offer. Running away from the problem, he went off to be a guest at the Château Montredon, near Marseille, where a Parisian patron of the arts, the Comtesse Pastré, offered free accommodation to needy young artists.

Then suddenly, in May, news came that *Sinfonia Sacra* – often in the future to be the work that would introduce Panufnik's music to new audiences – had won first prize (out of 133 entries from 38 countries) in a competition sponsored by Prince Rainier of Monaco for which he had anonymously entered it. A telephone call, and Camilla sped down from London for a month of general celebration on the coast near Menton.

Another tiny cottage near Farnham was Panufnik's base when he got back to England, but this time he took it with a clear awareness that he would not be there for long. Camilla's grandmother had owned a beautiful house on the banks of the Thames in Twickenham (twenty minutes' drive from the centre of London), and had left it to the local inhabitants on condition that it be used as a private dwelling. Camilla's parents now bought the lease, and the house was put at the couple's disposal for a peppercorn rent. On 27 November 1963 they were married.

Andrzej and Camilla Panufnik were married at Caxton Hall, London, in 1963.

Panufnik's first attempts at composition date back to 1923. Now, after forty years of war, bereavement, emotional turmoil, financial worries, and political oppression, he found himself leading

a kind of ideal existence I had only imagined, never experienced before in my life. I never had to answer the telephone, hardly even open any letter. Delicious meals were put before me three times a day without my having to spare even a thought in advance.

Extensive repairs were needed to put Riverside House itself in habitable condition, so the Panufniks lived temporarily in a small cottage in the grounds. Thus the first Twickenham composition, a choral commission titled *Song to the Virgin Mary*, was actually written in the eighteenth-century St Mary's Church a few yards along the river. It was the first piece Panufnik dedicated to Camilla, but fully two-thirds of the thirty works he wrote – all at Riverside House – in the next twenty-eight years would carry the same simple superscription, 'To my wife', or its equivalent.

Rather like high-fidelity equipment, which is better the less you notice it, a satisfactory life for a composer is one lived as far as possible without incident. All the more is this so for a composer like Panufnik. An intensely shy man, he hated public appearances, and consistently refused invitations to teach or lead workshops. Even discussing his work was anathema to him. He just wanted to be left in peace to write it. There was, he felt, altogether 'too much talking about music', and the programme notes he habitually supplied for his new works were a form of self-defence – his thoughts set down on paper 'so no one needs to ask me again'. With the routine that Camilla now established for him and maintained for the rest of his life, Panufnik was lucky enough to exchange becoming for being. Henceforth indeed his biography tells itself best in the unfolding of his output, as documented in the classified list of works.

But freedom means responsibility. Panufnik was very far from taking things easily from now on with his composing method, nor did a sudden spate of pieces come from his pen. On the contrary, apart from a flute-and-strings arrangement of *Hommage à Chopin* and another in his series of old Polish refurbishments (*Jagiellonian Triptych*), the next three years produced only one short new

Stokowski conducting a midnight recording of Panufnik's *Universal Prayer* at Westminster Cathedral, London, in 1970

composition, the seven-minute orchestral *Katyń Epitaph*. Meanwhile, Panufnik was using his new security as an opportunity of coming radically to grips with the problem of musical language to which *Tragic Overture* in 1942 had been one of his first responses and with which he had been grappling empirically ever since.

That problem is how to reconcile the demands of structure with those of expression; how (putting it another way) to combine mathematics with poetry. Within that formulation, the conflicting needs of unity and variety have also perennially occupied composers' attention. And with the enlargement and widespread breakdown of traditional concepts of key since the late nineteenth century, another specific new question has added itself to the old ones: how to respond to these evolutionary processes, manifested clearly in the work of Schoenberg and his followers, without confounding those generally acknowledged priorities of ear and mind that the anti-atonalist Ernest Ansermet addressed in his treatise on *The Foundations of Music in Human Consciousness*.

Panufnik's answers to these questions never became final answers, because a creative artist is an explorer, and can never solve the problems of art permanently. But from the biographical point of view, he made what he regarded as his essential breakthrough in two works of the late 1960s. In 1968 came *Reflections*, a technically taxing twelve-minute piece for solo piano premièred in London four years later by John Ogdon. *Universal Prayer*, the most tautly organized work Panufnik had yet produced, was begun the same year and completed in 1969. Thirty-two minutes long, scored for the unconventional combination of four solo voices, chorus, three harps, and organ, and based on the poem by Alexander Pope (another A. P. who had lived by the Thames, a few hundred yards along from Riverside House), it makes arduous demands on the listener's concentration by virtue of its own unrelenting structural rigour. But when Stokowski saw the sketches during a visit to Twickenham in the summer of 1968, the music immediately seized hold of his imagination: he insisted that Panufnik reserve the first performance of *Universal Prayer* for him, and he duly conducted it in the Cathedral of St John the Divine in New York in May 1970.

In spring 1968 the Panufniks' first child, Roxanna, was born, and their son, Jeremy, arrived thirteen months later. Agreeing as he did with a principle enunciated in another poem by Pope, 'Order is Heav'n's first law', Panufnik himself was struck by the advent of a 'new line of compositional progeny' at the same time as that of his children. The family was now complete. The musical language, though not definitive, had become a stable, practical tool he could go on using in a great variety of ways in the stability of the home that Camilla, while working productively as a photographer and writing many articles and books, continued to organize for him. She provided texts too for several of his vocal works, including a peasant song he wrote for the Kenneth MacMillan ballet *Miss Julie* in 1970. Other notable ballets to Panufnik's music have been choreographed by Martha Graham, Paul Mejia, and David Bintley; one of the finest of all was Gray Veredon's *Bogurodzica*, a worthy visual counterpart to the gestural strength of *Sinfonia Sacra* premièred by the Ballet de l'Opéra de Lyon in 1983.

Panufnik's composing, once beset by so many distractions, now proceeded copiously and calmly. The working method, once he embarked on a new piece, was simple and uniform. First, just as in Paris back in 1938 with Symphony No. 1, he had to 'find the

The conductor Georg Solti
(left) talks with Panufnik
between rehearsals
for the Chicago Symphony
Orchestra performances in
1992 of *Sinfonia Sacra*.

architecture' – a process facilitated by his new technical fluency, but still needed to establish the unique character and shape of each work. This was not a paper exercise: it was mostly done on riverside walks in the morning, or during long afternoons and evenings of thought in the old stable in the garden, which had now been converted into a comfortable studio.

During this stage of composition, Camilla knew that any social engagements were out of the question. But once the structural nut was cracked, and the outline of the work then roughly sketched in pencil, another side of Panufnik emerged. With all his moral and intellectual seriousness, his Polish dignity and courtliness, he could be a thoroughly boisterous man, with a vivid sense of humour that emerged both in hearty explosions of laughter and in an infectiously sly titter. He also loved good eating and drinking. So when he passed to the phase of actually writing a score out on paper, intense and concentrated work though this was, there would be – in addition to concerts – occasional highly spirited evenings or lunches with friends both musical and otherwise. The composition process itself remained obsessively private: not even Camilla was allowed to see a piece before it was finished. (Stokowski had been a privileged exception when he was allowed a glimpse of *Universal Prayer* in progress.)

The new works multiplied, in a wide range of forms. In 1971 Yehudi Menuhin commissioned a violin concerto. In 1973 (ten years after the composition of *Sinfonia Sacra*) the Sinfonia Concertante, Panufnik's fourth surviving work in the genre, heralded a rapid expansion in his symphonic series: *Sinfonia di Sfere* came in 1974–5, *Sinfonia Mistica* in 1977, and *Metasinfonia* in 1978. Spaced whenever possible between compositions were holiday trips abroad, often to Mediterranean regions, and a continuing succession of conducting engagements. The City of Birmingham Symphony Orchestra asked him back for two performances of *Sinfonia Sacra* during his seventieth-birthday season. A particularly cordial relationship was established with the London Symphony Orchestra. Having first played under Panufnik long ago, at an Albert Hall charity concert for Polish émigrés back in 1954, it recorded several of his works in 1970 with Jascha Horenstein and later with David Atherton. The LSO also commissioned works for various celebratory and competition purposes, invited Panufnik on several occasions to conduct, and

Yehudi Menuhin, who commissioned Panufnik's Violin Concerto, rehearses with the composer for the work's première at the 1972 City of London Festival.

marked his seventieth birthday with a concert at the Barbican Hall in London at which he conducted his Piano Concerto and *Sinfonia Votiva* (the latter commissioned for the centenary of the Boston Symphony Orchestra in 1982).

One of the commissions that gave him particular pleasure and pride was from the Royal Philharmonic Society. For its 175th-anniversary season in 1986–7 the Society – which had commissioned Beethoven's Ninth Symphony – now commissioned Panufnik's. Not surprisingly, he decided that the time had come to designate the new symphony by number, keeping its name, *Sinfonia di Speranza* ('Symphony of Hope'), for a subtitle. The 1982 Boston commission, and performances of *Sinfonia Sacra* by Sir Georg Solti and the Chicago Symphony Orchestra in the same year, had meanwhile sparked a resurgence of American interest in Panufnik's music. The Koussevitzky Music Foundation commissioned *Arbor Cosmica*. Its 1984 première in New York led to several further performances there and, in 1989, the commissioning of *Harmony* by the 92nd Street Y concert series, while other major commissions came from the Polish–American community of Milwaukee (a concerto for the bassoonist Robert Thompson) and the Chicago Symphony Orchestra (the Tenth Symphony).

In Poland, all this time, the atmosphere was changing by degrees. First professional publications were permitted to mention the names of expatriate artists like Panufnik again. Then, in 1977, came the first public hearing of his music in his native country for twenty-three years: a performance of *Universal Prayer* at the Warsaw Autumn Festival. The following year the visiting Scottish National Orchestra under Sir Alexander Gibson played *Sinfonia Sacra* at the festival, where it received a standing ovation, and Panufnik performances have become increasingly frequent both in Warsaw and elsewhere in Poland since then. His admirers in Poland organized invitations for Panufnik himself to come back and conduct in Warsaw. But it was not until democratic government had finally been restored through free elections that he agreed to return: on 16 September 1990, at the opening concert of the Autumn Festival, he conducted the European première of his Tenth Symphony.

Panufnik's late years brought him honours from all over the world.

Sir Andrzej Panufnik with his family at Buckingham Palace, London, after receiving a knighthood in 1991

On his triumphant return to Warsaw after his long years of exile, Panufnik talks with Lutosławski at the 1990 Warsaw Autumn Festival.

In London, he received the Sibelius Centenary Medal in 1965. Having won the first Prince Rainier Prize in Monaco with *Sinfonia Sacra* in 1963, he was again the first composer to receive it when it was changed to an award for a lifetime's œuvre in 1983. With all his international successes, he was no less interested in the musical life of his corner of England. *Thames Pageant* and *Winter Solstice* had both been written for local performing groups, and their composer was frequently to be seen in the audience at neighbourhood musical events of no grandeur at all.

In the New Year's Honours for 1991, Panufnik was created a Knight Bachelor. Everything seemed prosperous with the 76-year-old composer. But he was already ill with cancer. It was with difficulty that he fulfilled his last conducting engagement, recording his Ninth Symphony and Piano Concerto with the London Symphony Orchestra in June 1991. A commission to write a chamber work for the Nash Ensemble had to remain unfulfilled. The last work Panufnik wrote was the Cello Concerto, yet another London Symphony Orchestra commission (his third), this time for Mstislav Rostropovich. In September 1991, sitting wrapped in a blanket in the garden he loved, Panufnik showed me the completed score. But within an hour or so, he was tired. We said goodbye, and he went to bed.

On 27 October 1991, Sir Andrzej Panufnik died in Twickenham, aged seventy-seven. The President of Poland, Lech Wałesa, awarded him, posthumously, the Knight's Cross of the Order of Polonia

Restituta. There were two memorial concerts in London. The first, given by the London Symphony Orchestra at the Barbican in June 1992, included the Tenth Symphony and the première of the Cello Concerto. The second was given at the Queen Elizabeth Hall that October by the chamber orchestra London Musici, conducted by Mark Stephenson, a gifted young exponent of Panufnik's music whom the composer had proposed to conduct *Arbor Cosmica* at the 1989 Warsaw Autumn Festival.

Stephenson later took his orchestra to Warsaw for a Panufnik memorial concert for Polish television and radio, and they have made several Panufnik recordings for the Conifer label. Besides three Panufnik works and one of his favourite Mozart symphonies, their Queen Elizabeth Hall programme included a piece for mezzo-soprano and strings commissioned by the Park Lane Group for the occasion from Roxanna Panufnik, by then in her early twenties and herself established as a successful composer.

One good thing about being a composer is that your work continues to sound after you fall silent. With interpreters like Stephenson and the equally dedicated American conductor Gerard Schwarz left to play his music, and a daughter going on to write her own, perhaps that is doubly true for Panufnik.

2

Lutosławski became a much
sought-after conductor of
his own music from the
1960s onwards.

*I try never to lose sight of my basic aim – which
is to compose the particular aesthetic experiences
of my listener ... I am perfectly well aware
that my imagined listener is no typical listener,
and that he is even probably very particular.
For my work, however, he has one invaluable
advantage: he is the one listener about whom I
really know something. As such he is an element
absolutely necessary for me in composing music
– since it would be impossible for me to
imagine this process other than in conjunction
with a constantly imagined percipient of the
work. In this way creation and perception
intermingle and are elements of the same
complex phenomenon.*

Witold Lutosławski, *The Composer and
the Listener*, 1971

Witold Lutosławski

Lutosławski was born, like Panufnik, in Warsaw. He lived roughly the
same length of time as his slightly younger compatriot, and until 1954
the outward circumstances of their lives were broadly similar. They
were educated in the same conservatoire, and went through the Nazi
occupation together as friends and colleagues, brought together by
their activities as an underground piano duet. After the war they
suffered alike from the experience of a second invasion (this time, as
Panufnik put it in his autobiography, 'more psychological than
physical'), and from the constraints the Soviet-dominated regime
placed on their creative work.

Then in 1954 the two men's paths diverged: Panufnik fled Poland
in protest against the system, spending the rest of his career in exile,
while Lutosławski stayed and did his best to cope with that system

The young Witold
Lutosławski in 1917

from within. In such cases – the somewhat comparable decisions of Toscanini and Furtwängler twenty years earlier come readily to mind – it is all too easy for outsiders to deliver resounding moral opinions on the contrasting responses to reality. But looking back now on two long, often tormented, and in the end immensely fertile lives, we can see that the turning-point of 1954 was not merely circumstantial: what these two great men did tells us something fundamental about the difference in their characters. And it is worth noting that from the moment of Panufnik's departure from the Polish scene, Lutosławski's career took off in a manner previously unimagined by most of his colleagues.

Witold Lutosławski was born on 25 January 1913 into a background of social eminence and impressive cultural and intellectual achievement. His mother, Maria (née Olszewska), was the daughter of a landowner who taught mathematics; she studied at universities in Zurich, Berlin, and Kraków, and became a doctor. His father, Józef, was born in 1881 (a year after Maria). Józef's brothers included a philosopher (married to a Spanish poet and novelist), an editor who specialized in agricultural subjects, and a doctor-priest. At a time when their region of what we now call Poland languished under an earlier Russian domination, the brothers were all involved in nationalist politics. Several family members were musically gifted too: though Józef was never a professional musician, he is said to have studied the piano with the German virtuoso Eugen d'Albert, a protégé of Liszt.

Years later, Witold still remembered hearing his father playing Beethoven and Chopin 'very musically'. But he was not destined to enjoy such experiences for long. Józef and his brother Marian were undone by their political activism. Polish nationalist strategy had seen imperial Russia as a potential ally against another oppressor, Germany. Józef and Maria, with Witold and his two elder brothers, Jerzy and Henryk, naturally fled to Moscow as a refuge from the German advance in World War I. Then the 1917 October Revolution led to an accord – foreshadowing the Hitler–Stalin Non-Aggression Pact twenty-two years later – between Germany and the new Bolshevik state. Józef and Marian were arrested for 'counter-revolutionary activities', taken to a prison in Moscow, and executed without trial on 5 September 1918.

Following page, German infantrymen march through a Galician village in June 1915; operating against the Russians with a total force of close to four million soldiers, the Germans rapidly overran Poland.

From then on Maria Lutosławska, supported by other members of the two highly cultivated families, was responsible for bringing up Witold and his brothers, and in 1919 they settled in Warsaw. There, at the age of six, Witold took the first serious steps in his musical education. He began piano lessons with Helena Hoffman, and two years later, when his mother moved to the family estates around rural Drozdowo, continued with a local teacher – writing, like Panufnik, his first piano piece when he was nine.

Maria and her children moved back to Warsaw in 1924. Entering the Stefan Batory *gimnazjum,* Witold now also started to study with one of the city's best-known piano teachers, Józef Śmidowicz. It was at this time that the boy had his first encounter with modern music. He was 'dazed' by the experience of attending the Polish première of Szymanowski's Third Symphony (*Song of the Night*), and recalled later: 'Afterwards I ran home and spent days trying to recapture those sounds at the piano. For weeks I could think of nothing but this work'. But then 'came a strong reaction against the whole somewhat over-delicate aesthetic of that period, and my work never again showed the direct influence of Szymanowski'.

After beginning piano lessons as a boy, *above,* and studying harmony, counterpoint and fugue with Witold Maliszewski in his teens, Lutosławski entered Warsaw University, *right,* for two years of mathematical studies.

Another instrument had meanwhile begun to exert its attraction: in 1926 Witold began six years of violin lessons with Lidia Kmitowa, a former pupil of the great Joseph Joachim. In 1927 he wrote two violin sonatas ('terribly naïve' pieces, he found them in hindsight), and in the same year he entered the junior department of the Conservatoire, only to find – again like Panufnik – the pressure of combined high-school and music studies too much for him. But before leaving the Conservatoire in 1928 he had completed a Skryabinesque *Poème* for piano that was good enough to persuade Witold Maliszewski, who had studied with Rimsky-Korsakov at the St Petersburg Conservatoire, to accept him as a private pupil.

With Maliszewski, Lutosławski studied harmony, counterpoint, and fugue, but (as he said later), 'in a very concise fashion. I never studied those subjects thoroughly'. On the subject of form, on the other hand, Maliszewski was demanding in the extreme, requiring a totally concentrated approach towards music material and the elimination of every inessential note. It was presumably from Maliszewski, too, that Lutosławski was learning (as Panufnik was to under Sikorski's tutelage) to frame his compositions from the start in orchestral terms rather than as piano scores. Under this regime his first publicly performed piece, *Dance of the Chimera* for piano, was composed in 1930. He wrote a Scherzo for orchestra in the same year, and a set of incidental music for Janusz Makarczyk's *Haroun al Rashid* in 1931.

After concluding his *gimnazjum* studies in 1931, Lutosławski began two years of mathematics studies at Warsaw University. But when Maliszewski was appointed professor of composition at the Conservatoire the following year, Lutosławski joined his class there. At the same time, on Maliszewski's advice, he abandoned the violin to enter Jerzy Lefeld's Conservatoire piano class. Finally, in 1933, he gave up the attempt to combine mathematics with all his other studies and left the University.

The first orchestral performance of a Lutosławski work – as a pianist, he had already played his *Dance of the Chimera* at a Conservatoire concert in 1932 – soon came when Józef Oziminski conducted the Warsaw Philharmonic in a revised version of some of the *Haroun al Rashid* music. (The composer later preferred to regard the April 1939 broadcast première of his Symphonic Variations by

Among the musicians who founded the 'Young Poland' group in 1906, the conductor Grzegorz Fitelberg became the leading champion of works by his contemporaries and juniors for nearly half a century.

Grzegorz Fitelberg and the Polish Radio Symphony Orchestra as his real orchestral debut.)

The compositional output of Lutosławski's student years includes the first of his works to have survived, albeit only in manuscript: an ambitious three-movement Piano Sonata, completed on 29 December 1934. He gave several performances of it the following year (two of them at student exchange concerts in Riga and Vilnius), and broadcast it on Warsaw radio in 1938. Manuscripts of most of the other compositions of this period have disappeared, some in the 1944 Warsaw Uprising.

The Symphonic Variations, begun in 1936, took two years to complete. Lutosławski wrote the piece without his teacher's help, and his description of Maliszewski's reaction when he eventually saw the score, recounted to Varga, mirrors Panufnik's experience with Sikorski:

He declared openly that he did not understand it. I prepared the harmonic analysis of the piece – and he said: 'Now we talk a common language, now I understand it. But that does not mean that I like it. For me your work is simply ugly'. He added that if I developed along those lines, he would not be able to give me advice. – He was a wise and sincere man. He did not say the piece was bad, he just remarked that he did not like it. I respected him highly for that, after all my style was completely alien to him.

Meanwhile Lutosławski had written two movements on texts from the Requiem Mass for his composition diploma in 1937: a choral and orchestral *Requiem aeternam* (never performed, and now lost), and a *Lacrimosa* for soprano and orchestra with optional chorus, which was given its première in Warsaw in 1938 and recorded years later under the composer's direction.

Nearly two years older than Panufnik (who, as we have seen, went through his compositional studies in half the officially required time), Lutosławski thus graduated as a composer a year later. He had already graduated as a pianist in 1936. Back in those days there was evidently a discrepancy between the way the world (exemplified in Panufnik's account of their graduation quoted in the previous chapter) saw Lutosławski – essentially as a performer – and the way he saw himself:

I always regarded myself as a composer, I never thought of making my living as a pianist or a violinist. I knew I would be a composer who might also work as a performer.

'Until the outbreak of the war', Lutosławski told Varga, 'I spent my time preparing for a study trip to France'. But then, in September 1939, came the German assault on Poland. Lutosławski, already an officer cadet in a radio communication and signals unit in Kraków, now became an active combatant. The signals unit in which he served retreated to the Lublin area, and he was soon captured by the Germans in the course of their lightning invasion of western Poland. After eight days, he and some companions escaped while being marched through forest country by their captors, and walked 250 dangerous miles cross-country back to Warsaw; friends had also brought his mother there from Drozdowo, which was on the Soviet side of the agreed demarcation line. Ironically, given the Poles' traditional view of Russia as a natural ally, Witold's brother Henryk was unluckier in being captured by the Red Army: transported as slave labour to the Gulag Archipelago, he died there the following year of typhoid aggravated by starvation.

In Warsaw there now began a period as problematic for Lutosławski as it was for Panufnik, and one in which the two men were closer than at any other time in their lives. Panufnik shared accommodation for a while with the writer Stanisław Dygat, whose sister Danuta was later to marry Lutosławski. And at Panufnik's suggestion the two composers formed a piano duet. From among the works – more than 200 – that they adapted for café or underground performance over the next four and a half years, only Lutosławski's Variations on a Theme of Paganini (an arrangement of the Italian virtuoso's Caprice No. 24 for solo violin) has survived. Lutosławski also appeared with singers from time to time: in 1941, with the soprano Ewa Bandrowska-Turska, he gave the first performance of the two songs he had written seven years earlier.

Such activities provided Lutosławski – and his mother, who was now dependent on him – with a livelihood of sorts, but inevitably he managed to finish few new compositions during the war. Apart from a pair of piano studies, a woodwind trio, and a set of *Songs of the Underground Struggle*, much of his compositional effort went into a

Little more than seven weeks after the outbreak of World War II on 3 September 1939, Hitler was taking the salute at a march-past of light artillery in Warsaw.

Lutosławski stands on the right, Panufnik on the left, with the distinguished Polish poet Jarosław Iwaszkiewicz (1894–1980) in the centre; this picture of the three friends was taken around 1944.

series of fifty contrapuntal studies for various small woodwind combinations. Designed as 'laboratory' work rather than as concert pieces, they served as sketches for his major creative project of the time, the First Symphony, begun in 1941. The first movement was completed by 1944, but it took Lutosławski several more years to finish the remaining three to his satisfaction.

The course of Lutosławski's life during the nine years between the end of the war and 1954 can best be described as 'lying low'. There were a few notable performances. In September 1945 his Woodwind Trio was premièred at a festival of new Polish music held in Kraków together with the first Congress of the newly-founded Union of Polish Composers (of which he was elected secretary-treasurer). A Paris performance of the Symphonic Variations in December 1946 afforded the composer his first hearing abroad, and the work was played twice in Kraków in October 1947.

On 26 October 1946, Lutosławski married Maria Danuta, née Dygat, who since their meeting early in the war had studied architecture, and who had been married for a while to the architect

Jan Bogusławski, by whom she had her only child. The Lutosławskis lived for more than twenty years (with the composer's mother till her death in 1967) in a cramped flat in the Warsaw suburbs.

In 1946 Lutosławski had also conducted in public for the first time, leading the Katowice orchestra at Fitelberg's invitation in Haydn's 92nd Symphony. It was not until the 1960s, however, that he began to conduct his own music with any regularity, and he certainly had no intention of pursuing the kind of conducting career that at this time was diverting Panufnik from the central business of composing.

During the first postwar years Lutosławski's name, as Steven Stucky puts it in his perceptive book on the composer's music, 'came little by little to the fore', after a period when 'others – Panufnik, for example – seemed more promising'. Certainly, if we look at the honours and appointments Lutosławski received while Panufnik was still in Poland, it seems clear that the younger man enjoyed the greater prominence. In 1949, when Panufnik's *Sinfonia Rustica* took first prize in the Warsaw Chopin Competition, Lutosławski's Pushkin setting *The Snowslide* was winning second prize in a competition held to mark the 150th anniversary of the poet's birth. Panufnik, again, was awarded the Standard of Labour, First Class, in 1949 and was State Laureate in 1951 and 1952; Lutosławski's State Prizes came in 1952, 1955, and 1964. Nor were there for Lutosławski, despite his occasional trips abroad, any of those dubious diplomatic 'plums' such as Panufnik's vice-chairmanship of the UNESCO International Music Council, his study visit to the USSR in 1950, or his mission to China in 1953.

There were specific setbacks too. Lutosławski had finally completed his First Symphony in 1947, and Grzegorz Fitelberg gave the work its première with the Polish Radio Symphony Orchestra in Katowice on 6 April 1948. It was received with enthusiasm, one reviewer (the composer Roman Haubenstock-Ramati) greeting it as the first genuine symphony in Poland since Szymanowski's day. But by this time the Soviet-style 'Polish People's Republic' had come into being, and the Union of Polish Composers had formally accepted the 'socialist realism' line toed by their Russian colleagues. Before the end of 1948 Lutosławski was removed from the Union committee. (He was to rejoin it in 1951.) So it is hardly surprising that, after its Warsaw première the following autumn, his First Symphony was branded as 'formalist', and disappeared from Polish concert platforms for ten years. Significantly, a short Overture for Strings that Lutosławski wrote in 1949 was premièred by Fitelberg not in Warsaw but in Prague, and (as Stucky remarks) 'was to remain unheard in Poland for many years'.

The picture that emerges from all this is of a composer struggling to establish himself and his individuality, in inimical social circumstances, and somewhat under the shadow of a more obviously gifted colleague. A comparison of the two men's output at the time reinforces the two-tier impression. Between the end of the war and 1954, Panufnik wrote (or in two cases reconstructed) eight original works that were to take their place more or less prominently in his permanent repertoire. Over the same nine-year span Lutosławski produced an abundance of carol arrangements and songs (many of them for children), some instrumental pieces, incidental music and film scores, and the above-mentioned Overture; but only three works

Lutosławski leafs through a score at the piano in his study in Warsaw.

of the period – the *Little Suite* and *Dance Preludes*, and the more imposing Concerto for Orchestra – have retained much currency in today's concert halls (at least outside Poland), and even those three are based on folk-tunes and contain only a limited quantity of original thematic material.

What Lutosławski was doing, clearly, was what Panufnik had in mind when he described the writing of pieces like his *Old Polish Suite* and *Concerto in modo antico* as a pleasurable escape from political demands. It is only if we see Lutosławski's postwar activities in this light that we will be able to understand the pressure he was under, and the almost Machiavellian self-control that dictated his response to it.

At this point, the comparison between the two men becomes positively fascinating. Lutosławski allowed himself far less creative latitude than did his colleague. In all the interviews he was to give in later, more relaxed times, he remained absolutely consistent and convincing in his account of those years. There was 'functional' music, and there was 'serious' music. The 'serious' music was what he was really all about; the 'functional' pieces were a way of earning a living, and at the same time both an artistic safety-valve and a way of developing technique and language.

Lutosławski was quite clear that the folk elements were for him merely a convenience and a springboard – nothing like the source of inner creative stimulation folk music had been for Bartók. Even the Concerto for Orchestra, he has said, 'was not the music that I really wanted to compose. It was the music that I was able to compose; I was not ready yet to compose what I really wanted'.

This way of putting the point is instructive: 'I was not ready yet' – not 'I was not permitted'. Lutosławski's following remarks (quoted in Richard Dufallo's *Trackings*) are important enough to warrant quoting at some length:

> Some think that it was the pressure of the government that made me compose with folk-tunes. No! It's absolutely not true – a sheer misunderstanding! ... I began writing with folk stuff as a raw material as early as before the war ... It interested me, but never very profoundly ... How could they make me write something that they wanted? With a pistol at my head? No! So it's really ridiculous to say that ... It was sort of an episode. It served as something that replaced what I was not able to do

Highlanders from the
Zakopane region in the
Polish Tatra mountains
performing in folk costume

… When I was ready to realize my first examples as a result of my work on sound language, I just abandoned folk stuff, because it didn't interest me so deeply. So that was the end. In 1955 I got rid of it. Since then I have never used it.

In other words, the recourse to folk elements, and the composition of functional pieces that lay outside Lutosławski's primary creative aims, also helped him to realize those aims. At the same time, the tricky balancing act that political necessity did to some degree impose led to some unpleasant surprises. As Lutosławski told Varga:

I must say quite frankly that the guiding principles set out by the Minister of Culture on the formation of the assembly of the Composers' Union did come as a great shock to me. I broke down because I was afraid that the programme, outlined by the minister, would banish all my compositions to the drawer, up to the end of my life.

I had to make a living. I had to earn money. I never wrote anything that would have complied with the official requirements, but I was not averse to the idea of composing pieces for which there was a social need. (Children's songs, and so on.)

Later on, it was for those functional compositions of mine that the authorities decorated me because they mistakenly believed that I had composed them to obey the guiding principles. That was another shock

*because I realized that I was not writing innocent, indifferent little pieces,
only to make a living, but was carrying on an artistic creative activity in
the eyes of the outside world. [After this experience, Lutosławski gave up
writing children's songs till the political situation had changed radically
towards the end of the decade.]*

The novelist Anthony Trollope was fond of a proverb that
succinctly characterizes Lutosławski's dilemma: 'You cannot touch
pitch and not be defiled'. Like many of those characters Trollope
applies it to, Lutosławski thought he was acting for the best; but that
is not always the way life works out, especially in a People's Republic
on the Soviet model.

It was partly because he realized this, and partly because he could
no longer bear all the distractions and compromises imposed on him
by 1950s Polish life, that Panufnik made his seemingly unthinkable
decision and left. Ultimately, he was a boat-burner. And later, living in
England, he would say to Lutosławski when he saw him on one of his
visits, 'Oh, are you going back to the cage?'

Lutosławski was a different kind of person, better able to keep his
opinions and passions under control. There can be little doubt that he
preserved an inner integrity all through his life – and sometimes even
he was driven to outbursts of inconvenient candour by the 'deep
psychological depression' occasioned by the schizophrenic experience
of artists in Communist Poland. Early on, however, such outbursts on
his part seem to have resulted from the mistaken impression that, in
the context of some policy switch or other, speaking frankly was now
safe. It was not until the arduous days of the Jaruzelski regime in the
1980s that he felt his position strong enough to engage in
uncompromising protest on points of principle. On his impeccable
conduct during that period his reputation for courage largely rests;
and this courage seems to me all the more striking because, from
the occasions when I met him, the impression still remains of
an unfailingly civil and discreet man not framed to make
provocative pronouncements.

How far such character traits are reflected in Lutosławski's music is
discussed in Chapter 3. For the moment, we must take the narrative
beyond 1954, the pivotal year in his career. It was pivotal in two ways:
Panufnik defected on 14 July; and just eighteen days later Lutosławski,

This portrait of Lutosławski vividly conveys his intense seriousness.

after four years of work on the score, completed his Concerto for Orchestra. For Lutosławski, the consequences of the two events were intimately connected. After the première, given by the Warsaw Philharmonic Orchestra under Witold Rowicki's direction on 26 November 1954, Stefan Jarociński's review in *Przeglad kulturalny* was typical of the critical reaction: he concluded that the work established Lutosławski unequivocally as Poland's leading composer.

On all the foregoing evidence, it seems unlikely that such a conclusion could have been reached if Panufnik had remained in Poland. But Panufnik was now a non-person, and along the lines of 'the king is dead – long live the king!' a new cultural icon was needed in short order. The Poles were fortunate indeed that someone as gifted as Lutosławski should be on hand to assume the mantle, though it would be idle to deny that the circumstance was a lucky stroke for Lutosławski too. 'You are the only composer I have to fear', he once told Panufnik – a curious way, to say the least, of expressing one's relationship with a close colleague. In 1954, as if by magic, the threat was removed from the Polish scene, and it was from this moment that Lutosławski's list of national and international honours, and of international performances, accelerated out of all proportion to what had gone before.

Władysław Gomułka, First Secretary of the Polish Communist Party and a pioneer of liberalization, opens the party's 1959 congress, backed by gigantic portraits of Marx and Lenin.

The distinction just drawn – honours in and outside Poland, performances largely outside – is an important one. During the second half of the 1950s Lutosławski experienced something of the same schizophrenic response from the Polish authorities as Panufnik had before him: they were still more interested in letting composers win plaudits for their country through performances abroad than in exposing Polish audiences to potential infection by 'bourgeois formalism'. Despite his new status as top composer, and his election as moderator of the ninth General Assembly of the Union of Polish Composers in 1957, it was not until 1959 that Lutosławski's First Symphony could be heard again in Warsaw.

The wider political context was changing in these years, and arts policy changed with it. After Stalin's death in 1953, a gradual thaw had already begun, spreading from the USSR itself to the satellite countries. In October 1956, after eight years out in the cold, Władysław Gomułka was reinstated as First Secretary of the Polish Communist Party, to preside for a while over as much liberalization as could be managed without provoking a Russian crackdown. In the very same month, the Warsaw Autumn Festival was held for the first time as a celebration of international contemporary music.

Two years later the festival became an annual event. Every year since then, except for the martial-law year 1982, it has served both as a superb display-case for the work of Polish composers and as a place where Poles can keep up with creative developments in other countries. Witold Lutosławski was actively involved in the running of the festival, together with its initiators, the composers Kazimierz Serocki and Tadeusz Baird.

Like the overthrow of Nazism a decade earlier, Gomułka's 'Polish October' turned out to be an illusory rebirth of freedom so far as the wider social and political issues were concerned. Yet as long as Gomułka retained power or a semblance of it, a seemingly inexhaustible sequence of Polish composers seized the opportunity offered by the new atmosphere of creative freedom, at least twenty of them achieving some measure of international repute. Curiously, when the forces of political repression reasserted themselves, musical activity remained to some degree insulated from the deadening forces of collectivist art and 'social realism' that for a long time made the creative records of most of the Communist countries so dismal. And it

Lutosławski takes a bow with conductor Jan Krenz at the 1960 Warsaw Autumn Festival.

can scarcely be doubted that the musicians' privileged position stemmed in large part from the sheer prestige of the Warsaw Autumn Festival, the first avant-garde manifestation of international standing in any of the Soviet-bloc counties: attended year after year by practically every major composer from the West, it was a marketplace whose importance and world-wide visibility the authorities could not ignore, however much they may have disapproved of the ideas purveyed there.

In hindsight, we can perhaps see now that what was happening in Poland was the establishment instead of a different form of musical ideology – a tyranny, not of politically imposed collectivism, but of intellectually determined hypermodernism. Polish musicians had, in a sense, exchanged the influence of Moscow for that of Darmstadt. There, as early as 1946, the International Summer Courses for New Music had begun to assert an avant-garde orthodoxy that was to dominate the world composing scene until the 1970s, and in some places beyond.

Now that the borders were open again, Lutosławski himself – able for the first time in seven years to investigate current trends both through the Warsaw Autumn and on many trips abroad – was as thoroughly depressed by the new orthodoxy as he had been by the old:

*I was astonished [he told Varga] that everybody was composing in the
style of Webern. The period of imitating Webern's aesthetics and technique
culminated in 1959. I was on the jury of the Rome festival of the ISCM in
that year and had an opportunity to study a whole pile of manuscripts. I
felt very sad and lonely; if music was going to develop like that in the
future I would be left completely on my own.*

For the new generation of Polish composers, 1956 imposed the
same kind of task as had confronted the nineteen-year-old Hans
Werner Henze when in postwar Germany he had to absorb half a
century of musical developments previously suppressed by the Nazis.
Lutosławski, who had at least done some travelling in the late 1940s,
already knew more than his juniors, but for him too there was a great
deal of catching up to be done. In view of this, of the alienation he
felt from recent western developments, and of the generous way he
made himself available to younger composers for help and advice, it is
hardly surprising that he completed not a single new work – only an
orchestration of the 1954 *Dance Preludes* – in 1955 or 1956.

Public duties, too, welcome though they may have been when
they opened doors to new experience abroad, were coming to
absorb more and more of his energies. In the early stages of the post-
Stalinist thaw, he had already visited festivals in Helsinki (1955) and
Salzburg (1956). Increasing involvement with the ISCM took him to
Strasbourg in 1958 and Rome, as we have seen, in 1959; and in 1959 he
joined the organizing and programming committees of the Warsaw
Autumn. In just three months, between August and October 1959,
Lutosławski was elected to the ISCM's executive council, served on
a competition jury in Liège, and attended the contemporary music
festival in Donaueschingen.

In January 1959 the Union of Polish Composers gave Lutosławski
its annual prize (which he was to win again in 1973). But a more
significant award in the international context came in May of that
year, when he shared with Tadeusz Baird the first prize of the Tribune
International des Compositeurs of UNESCO. The work that won it
for him – the powerfully concentrated, intensely eloquent *Musique
funèbre* for string orchestra, dedicated to the memory of Béla Bartók –
had taken four years (from 1954 to 1958) to complete. Along with the
1957 Five Songs to texts by Kazimiera Iłłakowicz (whose comparable

General Wojciech Jaruzelski, who presided over the closing Communist years in Poland after the military takeover in 1981

Jan Krenz, the Polish
conductor who, Lutosławski
said, 'understands my
intentions best'

importance Stucky emphasizes), this was the piece in which
Lutosławski finally succeeded in escaping from folk sources and
creating for himself the first version of a really individual
musical language.

The *Funeral Music* was first performed at Katowice on 26 March
1958, under the direction of Jan Krenz (who among Polish conductors,
Lutosławski has said, 'understands my intentions best'). After a
triumphal performance at the second Warsaw Autumn six months
later, Stefan Jarociński movingly wrote:

> *One would have to be dull-witted and have film over one's eyes or
> envy in one's heart not to see what calibre of creative artist this is who now
> lives among us.*

Thus Jarociński's acclamation of Lutosławski as Poland's leading
composer, initially proposed after the première of the Concerto for
Orchestra, was reconfirmed in the context of a piece that the
composer himself approved of rather more enthusiastically. Apart
from the UNESCO prize, the *Funeral Music* rapidly brought
adherents to Lutosławski's cause all over the world: it received warm
ovations at the Venice Biennale and around the United States in 1959,
and by 1961 had been heard in London, Utrecht, Paris, Strasbourg,
Prague, Berlin and Basle.

It was at the following Venice Biennale, in 1961, that the next – and crucial – phase in the development of Lutosławski's musical language was unveiled. This took the form of a chamber-orchestra piece in a quite new manner, commissioned for the festival by the Polish conductor Andrzej Markowski, and titled *Jeux vénitiens* ('Venetian Games').

A set of orchestral pieces begun in 1958 had meanwhile run into creative problems. Eventually premièred in 1965, in Kraków, under the title Three Postludes, it stands as the composer's most puzzling work. In the useful short study *Lutosławski* that he edited in 1968, the Swedish musicologist Ove Nordwall spoke of the music's 'increasingly affirmative emphasis of the non-affirmative and unfinished and finally impossible – a private documentation of a profound stylistic crisis'. Thus perceptively described, the problem recalls Schoenberg's failure in 1932 to finish his opera *Moses and Aaron*. Endeavouring there to dramatize the conflict between the inarticulate idealist Moses (who communicates in a tortuous *Sprechstimme*, or heightened speech) and his glibly articulate poet brother Aaron (represented by the honeyed tones of a lyric tenor), Schoenberg faced the inherent conceptual impossibility of expressing Moses' victory in musical terms; after setting Moses' telling phrase *'O Wort, du Wort, das mir fehlt'* ('O word, thou word, that I lack') at the end of Act II, he found himself, inevitably, unable to go on, and the last act was never completed. In Lutosławski's case the dramatic element of the Moses–Aaron conflict was absent, but his problem – of how to reconcile the flowering of free musical organisms with the patterns of closed structure represented by conventional views of form – was equally insoluble within the fully determinate musical language he had hitherto employed.

John Cage, the American composer whose work exercised a powerful liberating influence on Lutosławski at a crux in his stylistic development

Aesthetic problems, however, for Lutosławski as for Schoenberg, were also opportunities. The impulse that resulted in *Venetian Games* came from the same experience that had undermined the Postludes: a chance encounter (as Lutosławski explained to Bálint Varga) with the music of John Cage through a radio broadcast in 1960:

It was in that year that I heard an excerpt from his Piano Concerto [i.e., Concert for Piano and Orchestra] and those few minutes were to

change my life decisively. It was a strange moment, but I can explain what happened.

Composers often do not hear the music that is being played; it only serves as an impulse for something quite different – for the creation of music that only lives in their imagination. It is a sort of schizophrenia – we are listening to something and at the same time creating something else.

That is how it happened with Cage's Piano Concerto. While listening to it, I suddenly realized that I could compose music differently from that of my past. That I could progress toward the whole not from the little detail but the other way round – I should start out from the chaos and create order in it, gradually. That is when I started to compose Jeux vénitiens.

It was at this point that Lutosławski's personal style took on its definitive general shape – a blend of fully determined pitch and overall form with 'indeterminate' elements of rhythmic freedom. To overlook the many refinements and further explorations in his remaining works – more than thirty of them – would be a fundamental error. But it is true to say that keeping a viable balance in the musical body politic between the forces of law and order and the impulses of libertarianism – between traditional bar-line notation and passages paced freely by individual players – remained the fundamental stylistic preoccupation of the last three decades of his life.

From the public point of view, the years after 1960 saw Lutosławski ascending steadily to what Charles Bodman Rae (who has written the most comprehensive book about his music) could accurately describe in 1993 as 'the pre-eminent position on the world musical stage that he occupies today'. The amount of sheer compositional hard work that went into gaining him such eminence is impressive enough in itself. Illustrative, too, of the difference in character between him and Panufnik is the way he was able to combine it with a relentlessly punishing schedule of other activities.

Lutosławski gave summer composition courses at Tanglewood, Dartington, and Aarhus, though he did no more teaching after 1968 – 'I am not good enough', he said later; 'there are others who are better suited for the job'. But as administrator and animator of the Warsaw Autumn, as counsellor to international organizations like the ISCM, as competition judge and mentor of young composers, as participator in panel discussions, as visitor to musical events around the world, and as conductor of his own music – in places as diverse as Aldeburgh (1965), East Berlin and Amsterdam (1971), Bydgoszcz, Leipzig, and Edinburgh (1972), Bucharest and The Hague (1973), Dublin and the Flanders Festival in Belgium (1978), the USSR and Japan (1979), and Turkey and Australia (1980) – he continued indefatigable. Clearly he had the ability to 'compartmentalize' that Panufnik lacked. He could separate his public persona from his ultimately private core of composing work, keeping both sides of his life active at the same time. And not surprisingly there is a similar duality of elements to be found in the music itself.

A seemingly inexhaustible sequence of honours and distinctions rewarded both Lutosławski's public services and his compositional achievements. Among them were honorary doctorates from a dozen universities and music schools, fellowships or memberships of academies in the United States and throughout Europe, and several more Polish prizes including – in the shifting political scene of 1984 – the Solidarity Award. Abroad, there were awards from governments, heads of state, and private institutions in Paris, Vienna, London, New York, Boston, Copenhagen, Helsinki, and Madrid.

The most important single honour, both for its inherent prestige and for the effect it had on his life, came when the University of

HRH Queen Elizabeth the Queen Mother, patron and president of the Royal College of Music in London, presenting Lutosławski with a Fellowship of the college in 1989

Lutosławski conducting at the
Warsaw Autumn Festival; he
was an influential figure in
the festival's development.

Louisville in Kentucky instituted its Grawemeyer Award in 1984. The idea of a composition award was nothing new, but the sheer size of the Grawemeyer *was*. Its monetary value of $150,000 meant that for the first time a prize intended for composers could actually enable them to live and work off its proceeds for a very considerable time. In 1985 Lutosławski was named as the first recipient of the Grawemeyer; characteristically, he announced in accepting it that he would use the prize money to set up a scholarship fund to enable young Polish composers to study abroad.

Commissions, meanwhile, were multiplying to the point where Lutosławski had to become highly selective in deciding what to accept, and he was developing creative partnerships with some of the greatest performers in the world. Down to 1960, most of his commissions and dedications were from and to Polish performers. Now he found himself commissioned by such institutions as the Swedish Radio (the String Quartet), the Salzburg Festival (the Piano Concerto), and orchestras from Amsterdam and London (*Mi-parti* and *Chain 1*) to Chicago (Symphony No. 3), San Francisco (*Chain 3*), Los Angeles (Symphony No. 4), and Saint Paul, Minnesota (Partita).

The composer rehearsing in 1989 with Lynn Harrell, a leading interpreter of his Cello Concerto

The cellist Mstislav Rostropovich not only inspired several major compositions for his instrument by Lutosławski, Penderecki, and Panufnik, but in his other career as conductor gave many performances of orchestral and choral works by the first two of the three.

The new vocal works of the 1960s and 70s, *Paroles tissées* and *Les Espaces du sommeil*, were written for singers of the calibre of Peter Pears and Dietrich Fischer-Dieskau, and the concertos of these and later years for Mstislav Rostropovich, Heinz and Ursula Holliger, Anne-Sophie Mutter, and Krystian Zimerman. The 1986 *Chain 2,* moreover, and the 1990 Interlude were both (like the Double Concerto for the Holligers) called into being by that inveterate commissioner of new music, Paul Sacher.

The roll-call of performers eager to associate themselves with Lutosławski is a dazzling assemblage of talent. In purely musical terms, too, the landmark compositions of his last thirty years achieved a reputation both wider and higher than anything the relatively simplistic Concerto for Orchestra or even the *Funeral Music* had gained for him in the 1950s. If it is fair to single out just a few works, then the *Trois Poèmes d'Henri Michaux* (completed 1963), the String Quartet, the Cello Concerto, *Mi-parti*, and the Third and Fourth

Symphonies may probably be ranked as those that marked the most decisive steps forward in style, status, or both.

In 1968 the Lutosławskis had left their uncomfortable flat in the Saska Kepa district of Warsaw for a much more spacious and elegant house of their own in Żoliborz. It was in this settled environment, and sometimes in Norway (where they also had a house), that the composer worked on his last pieces. For someone who had so emphatically established his credentials as a spokesman for freedom of thought in the Jaruzelski period, the overthrow of Communism in the final years of Lutosławski's life brought sweet relief from the pressures of an unconscionable political system.

Still full of creative projects for the future, he died on 7 February 1994, after suffering from cancer for several months. The obituaries that followed his death were broadly unanimous in estimating him

A 1991 portrait of Lutosławski in the study of his house in the Żoliborz district of Warsaw

A sketch by Roboz of
Lutosławski in rehearsal

one of the century's great composers. This judgment has been
supported by an impressive sequence of memorial concerts around the
world, and there is no sign of any diminution in the programming of
Lutosławski works or in the appearance of new recordings.

The Lutosławskis had been a devoted couple for more than forty-
seven years, Danuta's drawing skills coming often to Witold's aid in
the layout of complex scores. But like many gifted women who marry
composers, she had subordinated her own architectural and graphic
interests to her husband's career. For this reason, though it was a
further blow for the Lutosławskis' friends, her death just a few weeks
after his surprised no one. They usually travelled together.

Lutosławski described the compositional process itself to Bálint
Varga in a striking image:

> When I start work, it is as though I am flying over a city, and
> slowly losing height I can see more and more clearly the outlines, the streets
> and houses.

The inner motivation of a composer's (or at least this composer's)
life was among the broader subjects I discussed with Lutosławski in
March 1987, when he was in Philadelphia to conduct a programme of
his own music. Those conversations provided much of the
background drawn upon in this chapter. But it is perhaps a passage
from his own notebook, quoted to Varga in 1973, that best expresses
his feelings on this particular topic:

Artistic creative activity can be motivated by different aims. The most commonplace of these is the desire to attract the attention of others, to be popular, to earn money and so on. In my case, the main motive is the desire to give the most faithful expression of a constantly changing and developing world that exists within me. The question can be raised: am I only interested in what goes on in me and nothing else? Isn't this standpoint too introverted? My answer is: no. I have a strong desire to communicate something, through my music, to the people. I am not working to get many 'fans' for myself; I do not want to convince, I want to find. I would like to find people who in the depths of their souls feel the same way as I do. That can only be achieved through the greatest artistic sincerity in every detail of music, from the minutest technical aspects to the most secret depths. I know that this standpoint deprives me of many potential listeners, but those who remain mean an immeasurable treasure for me. They are the people who are closest to me, even if I do not know them personally. I regard creative activity as a kind of soul-fishing, and the 'catch' is the best medicine for loneliness, that most human of sufferings.

How far this inspiriting conception brought fulfilment for Lutosławski himself is a question admitting of more than one answer. A rather sombre conclusion is suggested by what he said when asked whether creation makes an artist happy:

It is ridiculous for someone to believe that happiness can be achieved on this earth. That is all I can say.

Expressed by a man whose actual music often seems so joyfully exuberant in its play of ideas and sonorities, such a saturnine attitude stands as one of those conundrums that make creativity the mysterious and inexplicable force it is. But how Lutosławski went about his 'soul-fishing' – the actual detail of the music, whether technical or secret – is an area of enquiry that allows more specific and verifiable responses. We have now reached the point where it is opportune to look for them, and to ask some further questions about the relations between self and art in composers as different as Lutosławski and Panufnik.

3

Three-note 'triads' in
kaleidoscopic permutations
are an essential element in
Panufnik's stripped-down
musical textures.

*In some compositions, I have allowed myself to
be dominated by a sense of geometrical pattern
and order: taking a single triad with its
perpetual reflections as my fundamental
structural element throughout a whole extended
work. However this stringent discipline of
constant repetition of reflected triads was not
chosen as a purely intellectual exercise
(construction for construction's sake), but rather
as a means to an end: as an aid to expression –
not a limitation of it. In all my works, I
attempt to achieve a true balance between
feeling and intellect; heart and brain;* impulse
and *design.*

Andrzej Panufnik, *Impulse and Design*, 1974

Panufnik and Lutosławski: Commentary

The central problem of music in the twentieth century has been the problem of finding a language. If a gulf has opened between contemporary composers and listeners, this is not because the former have run out of interesting things to say to the latter, but rather because a universally understandable way of saying them no longer exists. In addition to looking inside themselves to find what they need to express, composers have been forced to invent, as it were out of nothing, a new idiom for its expression. The means thus created have tended, in an artistically rootless era, to change radically from one work to the next, confronting audiences with the task of beginning all over again each time they try to respond to a new composition.

It is several hundred years since music faced a comparable difficulty. The last period of such far-reaching change was in the seventeenth century, when the modal polyphony of the high Renaissance gave place to the tonal harmony and counterpoint of the early Baroque. Fundamental musical values were then called so radically into question that Monteverdi, for example, cultivated two entirely different styles through much of his composing life, passing deliberately from one to the other as each new creative challenge dictated. The transition from Baroque to Classical style 150 years later was less disorienting to musicians and public, since this time the essential basis of the tonal language was not undermined, even though its resources and functions were greatly expanded.

In tonal music, at any given moment in a piece, and often broadly through a whole work or movement, one specific note of the chromatic scale asserts its quasi-gravitational pull over the other eleven, thus becoming a 'tonal centre' or 'key-note'. The predominance of sets of notes belonging to a given key (e.g., C, D, E, and so on when the key is C major) over the ones that lie between them (e.g., C sharp, E flat) leads to a style that is known as 'diatonic'. The vast extension of chromaticism – of the use of notes 'foreign' to the prevailing key – in the music of Wagner and his late-Romantic followers did by the beginning of the twentieth century put tonality itself in jeopardy. It brought music closer to a condition of atonality, in which – at least theoretically – no tonal centre is established, and no key is home.

This development gathered momentum around 1910 through the contribution of Arnold Schoenberg. The Schoenbergian rule, to put it over-simply, was that a given note should not be repeated until all the other eleven had been heard. The idea was to get away from the clinging influence of traditional tonality, by discouraging the emphasis of any one note at the expense of the others. The twelve-note (twelve-tone in American usage) method that Schoenberg thus created is one case of what Lutosławski has in mind when he speaks of 'total chromaticism'. It is sometimes called 'serial' technique, because Schoenberg, and many of his successors, tended to base each work on one specific formulation of the twelve chromatic notes, known variously as 'basic shape', 'note-row', or 'series'; another name for the technique is 'dodecaphony'.

The change in technical method drew added force from a questionable belief in historical inevitability. At the same time the spread of Freud's psychological theories was fostering a climate of thought that encouraged acceptance of pain, self-doubt, self-denial, and even neurosis as necessary elements in artistic experience. For several decades composers, dazzled by the combination of historical factors and dominated by the strength of Schoenberg's personality, embraced the darker side of human experience (which harmonized well with the shifting, rootless nature of twelve-note music) as if it were the only fit material for art. Pleasure, as an artistic principle, came to be seen as a cause not of joy but of guilt; and except in the work of a few exceptional individuals, beauty itself became a suspect word and an all-but-forbidden concept.

Since the end of the 1960s, signs that this phase has run its course have begun to proliferate. In one of those paradoxes that make the arts and their enjoyment so endlessly fascinating, the word 'modern' has itself come under suspicion and begun to denote a kind of music that is really rather old-fashioned. Senior composers once uncompromising in their rejection of tonal methods, like Peter Schat in Holland, Kurt Schwertsik in Austria, Peter Maxwell Davies in England, and Jacob Druckman in the

United States, have been among the many to readopt tonality in their recent works.

The relation to tonality is not the only indication of a composer's stance vis-à-vis modernism and tradition, though it tends to be a very informative one. Important also are his approach to questions of notation and the role of the interpreter and, in a wider sense, his attitude to previously existing music and to the crucial interplay between composer and public. It was through their contributions in all these areas that Panufnik and Lutosławski established themselves among the major creative figures of our time, and it is through the difference in their response to such issues that we can most clearly apprehend the individuality of each man.

If we start from their views of the supposed breakdown of tonality and of Schoenberg's reaction to that problem, the initial difference between Panufnik and Lutosławski seems obvious and wide enough. Panufnik, as we have seen, went to study in Vienna partly because he wanted to extend his knowledge of Schoenberg and his disciples, and hoped to study with Webern. Lutosławski saw his own line of descent in quite another light. He told Richard Dufallo in 1987:

> There's practically no trace of twelve-tone doctrine in my music. Even if I use some rows containing twelve different notes, I think the very idea of the twelve-tone row doesn't belong to Schoenberg exclusively. It was in the air. It's quite natural that total chromaticism is something which is a question of our time. It is a natural step in the development of music in our time. But I think the other source from the past is the Debussy tradition. Debussy-early Stravinsky-Bartók-Varèse, that's a sort of line to which I clearly belong.

This is all very well, but the matter is not so simple. Like Peer Gynt's onion, the reality begins to look different as we strip the outer layers off. Rather like Frank Martin, Lutosławski may be said to have juxtaposed twelve-note elements with others that sound tonal (though he rejected the 'tonal' label for his own music). But in contrast to Martin's case (and much more in line with that of Schoenberg himself), it was indeed the idea of total chromaticism – of consistently using all twelve notes of the chromatic scale as the foundation of his harmonic language – that remained cardinal in Lutosławski's stylistic evolution.

Panufnik, for his part, soon saw that he had to turn in a different direction. While still a student, he recounts in *Composing Myself*:

> *I could see what Schoenberg was attempting. I agreed with the principle of a self-imposed discipline, a limitation to achieve unity. However, judged from the standpoint of my own purposes, his method seemed to achieve unity only at the cost of the equally desirable goal of variety. The 'democratization' of the twelve notes of the chromatic scale seemed to block the way to essential expressive elements: the prohibition against note-repetition meant that, even if the composer succeeded momentarily in creating a certain expressive character by emphasising particular notes, he was immediately compelled to neutralize it by letting the others have their say ... I threw my dodecaphonic [twelve-note] sketches into my waste paper basket, and concluded that I should never again try to borrow methods from other composers.*

Lutosławski, it should be recognized, was as firmly determined as Panufnik on arriving at a language of his own: his fundamentally chromatic idiom was certainly not 'borrowed' from anybody. The point is rather that he was not troubled in the same way by the problem that sent Panufnik off on another route: the element of sameness – of colourlessness – that music risks when it allots strictly equal time to all the colours (or 'chromata').

In the 1990s 'political correctness' is as hot a general topic as chromatic serialism was on the 1930s musical scene. While this book was being written, Janet Daley observed in *The Times* that, 'carried to its inevitable conclusion, cultural relativism produces not tolerance but nihilism. If everyone is right, then no one is'. *Mutatis mutandis*, that is exactly what Panufnik perceived about 'democratizing' the notes out of which alone music can derive its character.

It was this perception that led Panufnik to his own stylistic solution. More and more rigorously from the *Tragic Overture* on, his works have come to rely for all their thematic material on one or two basic three-note configurations – 'triads' in a non-technical sense of the word – articulated in every possible way and transposed (moved up or down *en bloc*) to a wide range of pitches. The method produces a formidable, and entirely modern, sense of organic unity. Thus far, a bald description may suggest a parallel with Schoenbergian serialism.

What transforms the effect is, quite simply, the small number of the notes that make up his thematic cells. By eliminating from each more notes than he includes, Panufnik can create highly specific atmospheres, and, when he wishes, blend them in a wide variety of mixtures and proportions. The technique accommodates sound-complexes of any desired degree along the chromatic–diatonic axis. The consequent range of expressive connotation is of a different order from anything commonly yielded by the twelve-note serialism of the Second Viennese School.

So we are faced, again, with a paradox: through a procedure that is at root serial – the systematic deployment of specific thematic units – Panufnik was able to achieve the quite unsystematic goal of free poetic expression. In this regard, at least as far as aims are concerned, it would be invidious to try to draw a contrast between the two composers under discussion. Just as Panufnik always insisted,

> *for me personally music is an expression of deep human feeling …*
> *I never regard the technical side of a musical work as an end in itself,*

so Lutosławski emphasized that

> *inspiration is an indispensable precondition of the creation of an*
> *authentic composition … One composes because one feels a strong need to,*
> *but one knows at the same time that one has something to communicate*
> *to others.*

His description of creative activity as 'a kind of soul-fishing', quoted in the previous chapter, is in the same vein.

From such common starting-points, these two intensely humanistic and highly intelligent composers both arrived at a way of composing that facilitated expression through stringent control. Yet the difference in the effect their works respectively make on the listener could hardly be more extreme.

Panufnik, the product of a Catholic intellectual tradition incorporating a generous dose of continental metaphysics, writes from a sense of mystical oneness with nature: his very devotion to systems, like that of the medieval Schoolmen, stems from a consciousness that only through their controlling power can the chaos of the universe be brought within humanly manageable bounds. Where Panufnik is metaphysical, Lutosławski is empirical: looking outwards rather than inwards, he is the sophisticated, cosmopolitan man of reason, absorbing impressions from the multifarious phenomena of the world around him, and then imposing on them the discipline of his own formidable intellect.

The two processes sound much the same, but the core of the difference lies in what counts first and most – the diversity of the impulse, or its unifying action. With due allowance for exceptions, the consequence might be summarized in this way: a Panufnik work is impressively 'all of a piece', whereas a Lutosławski work is no less impressively a fusion of contrasting, even conflicting, elements.

It is this thought that brings us back to Lutosławski's ability – also touched on in the last chapter – to 'compartmentalize'. In the same way that he could combine for much longer than Panufnik the careers of composer and public man (and during the Communist period keep his real views and feelings more successfully private), in the same way that having written his music he could also lecture about it (a task Panufnik consistently shunned), so Lutosławski was able also to bring together in his works elements of musical language of a disparity that Panufnik would have found it impossible – indeed undesirable – to think of combining. He was a synthesizer at heart, as the penchant of his folk-based pieces for combining modal or tonal tunes with non-tonal harmony and counterpoint had already shown in the 1940s.

A proverb propagated by Isaiah Berlin after Tolstoy – and the Russians in their turn took it from the Greek fabulist Archilochus – has it that the fox knows many small things, but the hedgehog knows one big thing. On the basis of that formulation, Lutosławski must surely be counted as a fox, and Panufnik as a hedgehog.

How, it may be asked, does this picture square with Panufnik's stated reservations about a method that could achieve unity 'only at the cost of the equally desirable goal of variety'? Wouldn't he (if my application of Archilochus is right) be the one to risk excessive uniformity in his music? No, for it was precisely because he perceived this danger that Panufnik turned to three-note thematic cells instead of twelve-note rows. Thereby he achieved clearly-defined expressive character even within a technique that systematically rotates and transposes and inverts and permutates a stringently limited thematic

Lutosławski's *Variations on a Theme of Paganini* typifies the relatively traditional layout of his earlier scores. It was written in 1941 as material for his wartime piano duo with Panufnik.

vocabulary; and it was the definiteness of character that in turn facilitated variety, since it is vagueness, not definiteness, that inherently resists variation.

Conversely, it was Lutosławski's very acceptance of a totally chromatic and non-tonal harmonic language – 'Instinctively, I had always tended toward atonality', he once observed – that brought home to him the necessity of assuring variety in the face of chromaticism's homogenizing tendency. His response to this necessity took two directions.

In the harmonic sphere, he developed a way of ordering sounds in differentiated layers. One typical method was to take six of the twelve notes of the chromatic scale as the harmonic basis of a passage, and fashion the melody from the other six. Another resource was to distribute notes and intervals among contrasting instrumental groups: woodwind, brass, and strings may thus at any given moment be operating in quite different sub-areas of the 'chromatic whole'. Both, again, are examples of synthesis, fundamentally opposed to Panufnik's unitary method.

How far these devices achieve the *sense* of contrast and differentiation in the individual ear (as distinct from the knowledge gleaned through the score-reader's eye) is a question each listener must decide for himself. Lutosławski's American near-contemporary Elliott Carter has explored similar ways of distributing interval patterns among specific instrumental groups. My own feeling – a consensus on such matters can only come with time – is that, if you compare the two men's use of the technique, Lutosławski's tends to work better, because the interval patterns themselves often have a clearer individual character to start with.

But Lutosławski himself seems to have felt that something beyond these careful procedures was needed. For if you compose with a harmonic language that resists sharp expressive profiling, and you still want to create dynamic rather than static forms, then the dynamism has ultimately to come from some source other than the harmony.

It is interesting that in 1958, when one of his most compelling works, the *Funeral Music* for strings, had its première, Lutosławski observed:

> *What I have achieved in this work is a combination of means that permits me to move within the scope of twelve tones, outside both the tonal system and conventional dodecaphony ... This is my first word spoken in a language new to me, but it is certainly not my last one.*

In the face of this declaration, one would expect the language of *Funeral Music* ('the only piece', Lutosławski said, 'where I have used a twelve-note row methodically') to furnish the basis for much in the composer's subsequent development. Yet this is exactly what did not happen. The quasi-serial method of *Funeral Music* turned out to be the road not taken, despite the triumphant formal cohesion and the expressive vividness of the piece – perhaps not despite but actually because of them: for the impact of the work's climax seems like that of an irresistible force meeting an immovable object.

In evoking the feeling of loss appropriate to the commemoration of Bartók, what Lutosławski created here was a sense of immobility, of totally static frustration. Its achievement is a *tour de force* of rare potency. But *tours de force*, as Stravinsky discovered when *The Rite of Spring* was behind him, tend of their very nature to be unrepeatable. Wisely therefore, after attempting to extend the stylistic gains of *Funeral Music* in the work that was eventually left in the curiously inchoate form of the Three Postludes, Lutosławski decided that he was after something different.

What sparked the decision was as we have seen (in Chapter 2) the encounter with Cage. Once Lutosławski realized that full control by the composer of harmony, melody, and form could be combined with an aleatory (from Latin *'aleator'*, or 'dice-player') element of rhythmic freedom for the performer, he had the key to reconciling total chromaticism with variety. Virtually all the music he wrote from 1960 on, beginning with *Jeux vénitiens*, presents a double face: formidable overall control on the one hand, and longer or shorter stretches of executant freedom on the other.

It is curious that two men with such disparate aesthetic standpoints could make equally productive use of the same technical resource. Cage, himself a mystic at heart, was strongly influenced by the collectivist trend of Eastern philosophies: he regarded music's dominance by an overmastering creative personality as a form of arrogance, and consciously strove to eliminate it from his own – if the word 'own' is admissible – work. Lutosławski, on the other hand, never wished to abdicate overall control, and saw his use of indeterminacy merely as a way of attaining a fluidity of rhythmic effect that he could achieve by no other means. He insisted always that the variations from one realization of such sections in his music to the next were of local and minor significance, not fundamental as Cage wished such differences to be. And beyond their local effect, the interrelation of the *ad libitum* passages with the *a battuta* sections (those beaten by a conductor in the traditional manner) itself served to enhance the expressive range of the music in ways that could differ greatly from one piece to the next.

The listener who explores Lutosławski's mature output will encounter a correspondingly broad range of musical qualities, certainly striking and individual enough to justify the composer's exalted reputation. The surface of his work is as lustrous and brilliant as anything to be found in the music of our time. His handling of the orchestra was assured to start with, and grew breathtakingly so over the years. Certain melodic shapes, such as a mournful little chromatic group of notes turning tightly in upon itself, come to seem as characteristic and welcome in his music as the familiar turns of phrase of an old friend (rather like Verdi's favourite 'weeping' semitones, and some comparable motifs that recur in Bartók).

From *Venetian Games* itself to the Third Symphony (1981–3) and beyond, the sheer instrumental invention astonishes without ever resorting to eccentricity. Along the way, several works stand out as especially good introductions to Lutosławski's personality and manner. They include the Second Symphony (1965–7), with its volcanic textures and stertorous brass interjections (as well as the two-movement form he came increasingly to cultivate); *Livre pour orchestre* (1968), with its enigmatic aleatory interludes that function as 'breathing-spaces' for performers and audience; and *Mi-parti* (1975–6), whose fragile yet clearly focused sonorities have led many commentators, though not the composer himself, to regard it as his finest work.

In such pieces, the aleatory passages in particular afford the woodwind and brass sections latitude for much trenchant and highly original expression. But when Lutosławski writes for strings alone, as in the ambitious and formally ingenious Preludes and Fugue (1970–72 – at about thirty-five minutes, his longest work apart from the set of twenty Polish Christmas carols), the imagination he shows is hardly less noteworthy.

The addition of voices, in works like the *Trois Poèmes d'Henri Michaux* (1961–3), *Paroles tissées* (1965), and *Les Espaces du sommeil* (1975), further expands and also clarifies the music's expressive range. But for me it is the Cello Concerto of 1969–70 that stands as the most brilliantly realized of all Lutosławski's orchestral works, and, with the String Quartet of 1964, as his greatest achievement. The inbuilt double nature of the concerto medium offers the most natural arena for Lutosławski's duality of styles to play itself out upon, and in the case of this particular concerto the opportunity of writing for that arch-individualist Mstislav Rostropovich stimulated him to a new heightening of expressive pungency and a positively theatrical intensity and specificity of characterization. Improvisatory and determinate sections, personal emotion and group response, quirky wit and disquieting drama succeed and act upon each other here in a vertiginous and inexhaustibly provocative outpouring of invention. The result may seem zany at times, but there is always method in this exuberant music's madness.

Aleatory elements play a full part in the Cello Concerto, but it is the String Quartet that goes farthest of all Lutosławski's works in the aleatory direction – so much so that creating a score for the work on paper caused him considerable problems. Eventually his wife pasted strips of music together in a way that graphically highlights the extremely independent nature of the four instrumental parts. Writing about the String Quartet in 1980, Steven Stucky felt that 'the uncompromising nature of its musical language places it among the least readily accessible of his recent compositions'. My own experience differs, since I saw how instantly my daughter, then seven years old, took to the piece when I was flipping through channels on a car radio: 'Oh, let's listen to *this!*' was her immediate reaction.

It may be suggested in any case that perhaps the String Quartet is among Lutosławski's most cogent creations partly because it is one of the least mixed in style: the aleatory method dominates practically unchallenged. For (and here we come to the rub), despite the beautiful, suggestive, and often thrilling results Lutosławski achieved over a thirty-year span through his inexhaustibly inventive interweaving of total chromaticism with aleatory methods, there are certain drawbacks inherent in such a combination – and these indeed seem to have become more evident to him in later life.

In *The Music of Lutosławski* Charles Bodman Rae puts the point revealingly, without seeming quite aware of its significance. From about 1980 on, Lutosławski tended both to reduce the proportion of aleatory to precisely notated sections, and to retreat from the position of total chromaticism his harmony had hitherto adopted. Noting that 'only fifteen of the eighty pages of the score of the Fourth Symphony are devoted, either entirely or in part, to *ad libitum* co-ordination', and describing some carefully differentiated chords used in the work, Rae goes on to observe:

> *The outcome is radically different from the technique of deploying a*
> *twelve-note chord-aggregate [containing all the notes of the chromatic scale*

simultaneously] within an ad libitum section. The problem of harmonic stasis, endemic to many of Lutoslawski's earlier works that make extensive use of aleatory technique, is here overcome. As a consequence of maintaining metred control over the orchestra the composer is able to regulate not only the rhythmic pulsation but, more significantly, the pace and precise moments of harmonic change.

An unsympathetic reader could be forgiven for wondering at this point whether Rae's message about the chromatic–aleatory nexus in Lutosławski (like the conclusion of certain deplorable persons about democracy in political life) may not be: 'Oh dear, it was all a terrible mistake'. The enormous and well-informed enthusiasm of his book as a whole shows that he is *not* saying that, nor need we say it. The surface brilliance and atmospheric texturing of the music itself, as well as the impression it has made on general audiences and fellow-composers alike, are so remarkable that such a reproof would be idle. But the question does arise (and it is not a trivial one) whether the stylistically hybrid forms Lutosławski was for so long seeking to create can actually be achieved without inherent inconsistency.

With Panufnik the impression on the listener is very different. There is, for one thing, no surface in his music at all, but rather a sense of absolute homogeneity fusing invention and treatment, line and texture, content and form. If anything, you may occasionally feel that a given piece insists *too* schematically on its monolithic oneness of character. *Sinfonia Mistica*, for example, or *Metasinfonia*, or even that pivotal work in Panufnik's stylistic evolution, *Universal Prayer*, can in their granitic Parmenidean unity risk being heard as doctrinaire.

Mostly, though, the resource Panufnik had acquired by fashioning his materials out of strictly limited sets of notes enabled him to articulate controlled structure over an amply broad and many-shaded spectrum of expressive characters. Three-note or four-note cells function in his music rather like traditional tonality: shifting the 'triads' to new pitch levels produces an effect comparable to that of modulation, and combining them simultaneously at several pitches parallels the use of heightened dissonance in a tonal context. By means of this, the needs of contrast and intensification are simultaneously served.

Following page, Lutosławski's 1983 *Chain I* characteristically alternates strict overall control with stretches of relative freedom for the performers; the downward arrows and broken lines indicate approximate points of ensemble, not exact simultaneity.

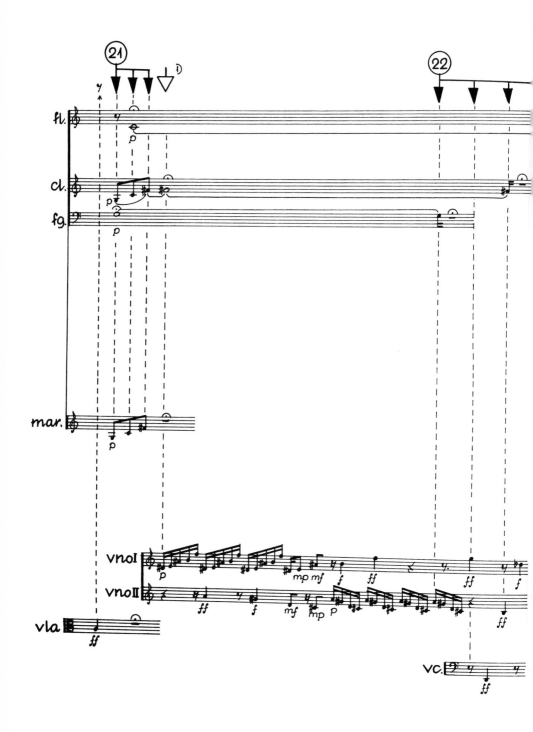

There is a further source of diversification, too, in Panufnik's inveterate use of geometrical, numerical, or other conceptual and visual models as a kind of scaffolding for his form. The symmetrical paper-cuts made by peasants in northern Poland furnished an image for the structure of works as widely separated in time as *Sinfonia Rustica* (1948) and the Third String Quartet (1990). Spheres and circles, in *Sinfonia di Sfere* and *Sinfonia Mistica* respectively, gave place to the spiral in *Metasinfonia*, the 'golden ellipse' in Symphony No. 10, and the mandorla of ancient religious art – the palindromic almond shape that results when two equal circles overlap – in the last work of all, the Cello Concerto of 1991. A more abstractly conceptual image, the fundamental dualism of Tantric philosophy, gave rise to *Triangles* (written specifically for television), and the later *Arbor Cosmica* sought to represent in sound the traditional artistic symbol of the cosmic tree.

Such pointers do not necessarily help an individual listener's comprehension of the piece in question, and Panufnik in his last years came to accept, if hesitantly, that it might in some cases be better to omit them – as a potential distraction – from programme notes. On the other hand, it is worth emphasising that each such image functions consistently as a pattern for the articulation of material

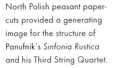

North Polish peasant paper-cuts provided a generating image for the structure of Panufnik's *Sinfonia Rustica* and his Third String Quartet.

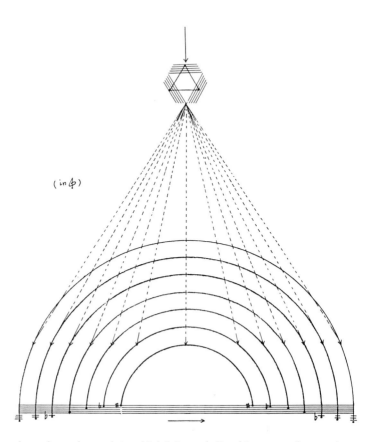

The choice of fundamental notes for Panufnik's Ninth Symphony was articulated through the idea of the rainbow and its prismatic effect.

throughout the work in which it is used. For this reason, the practice is not open to the criticism that may be levelled at Lutosławski's interleaved *ad libitum* passages – namely, that they inject an alien static element into forms that are by intention dynamic and mobile.

Only once, in the central section of *Autumn Music* (1962), did Panufnik essay the combination of two levels of 'fixedness' in tempo and texture, superimposing a semi-free (though closely controlled) acceleration and then deceleration in some instrumental parts over the unchanging tempo of another one. As we have seen (in Chapter 1), the device was precipitated by a programmatic image: a human life declining in autumn, while the passing of time is marked by the implacable striking of the clock.

It is doubtless no more than coincidence that *Autumn Music* and Lutosławski's *Funeral Music* are both memorial pieces; but they are certainly, in their opposite ways, exceptions to their composers' normal practice – and they also rank among the most emotionally satisfying works achieved by either. For a listener new to Panufnik's music, the immediate reaction to the sensuous chains of third-dominated woodwind chords in the outer sections of *Autumn Music* may well be astonishment that anything so disarmingly euphonious should have been attempted, let alone successfully carried through, in a century sparingly endowed with such musical voluptuousness. Yet, obviously, the piece could not have been written at any other time.

Autumn Music, like *Funeral Music*, is a one-off phenomenon in structural terms, though its trenchant concentration had been anticipated on a relatively small scale by the *Tragic* and *Heroic* overtures. The consistent core of Panufnik's œuvre by contrast, much more emphatically than in the case of our other three composers, is to be found in his symphonies. From *Rustica* to No. 10, they cover a creative span of forty years (which Nos. 1 and 2, had they not been lost in the Warsaw Uprising, would have extended to half a century), and they are all utterly characteristic of his artistic vision at the time of their composition.

Thus the *Sinfonia Rustica* of 1948, being an early work in Panufnikian terms, still partakes in its outer movements of what the composer calls 'quasi sonata' form, and it breathes a beguiling atmosphere deeply rooted in Polish folk art. Actually the third of Panufnik's symphonies in order of composition, the work shows at several points a spiritual affinity with the calm spaciousness of another folk-related, originally unnumbered, 'country' Symphony No. 3: Vaughan Williams's *Pastoral* of twenty-seven years earlier. At the same time, *Rustica*'s overall design is prophetically symmetrical, both formally and in physical layout – the two string orchestras are disposed 'stereophonically' at the sides of a small wind group.

Eloquent and accomplished though it is, the *Sinfonia Elegiaca* of 1957 must also be regarded as in some ways a work of less than complete maturity. Neither here nor in *Rustica* does the composer achieve or aim for the range of poetic evocation already covered in 1947 by both *Nocturne* and *Lullaby* (the latter a daringly original work whose neglect by the record companies is unaccountable). So it was in 1963, with *Sinfonia Sacra*, that Panufnik really hit his symphonic stride.

Opposite, a strong visual image of the 'cosmic tree' that provides its title is an integral element in the musical texture of Panufnik's Arbor Cosmica.

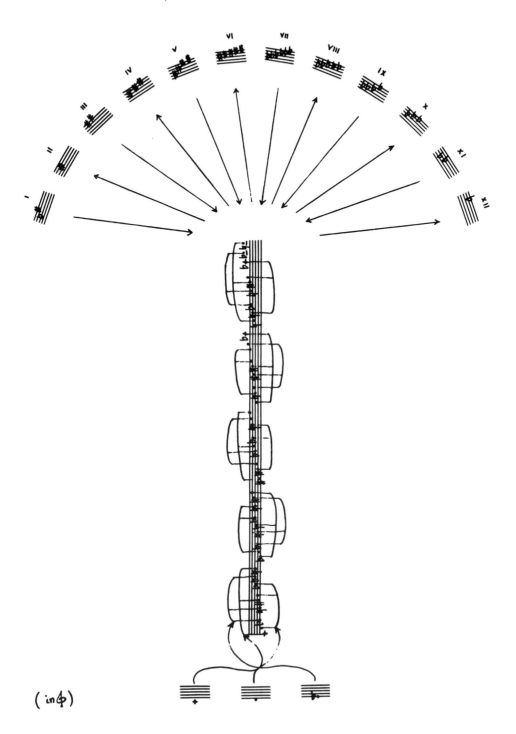

Appropriately for the work that transformed his career when it won the first Prince Rainier Prize in Monaco, *Sacra* has continued for four decades to be his introduction to diverse publics around the world, and it is worthy of the role. The essence of Panufnik is here. Rooted thematically in the *Bogurodzica* chant that had haunted him since he first heard it on the radio as a 21-year-old nervously awaiting his army medical, the symphony brings to this material (as the French critic Bernard Gavoty commented) 'the gift of incantation, of sorcery, without which music is only artifice'. Yet the elaboration of the material in symphonic terms is finely artificed too, and suggestive of Panufnik's thematic-cell technique: each of the three Visions that make up the first movement is based on one specific interval of *Bogurodzica*, which is then treated with cumulative breadth as a melodic whole in the concluding Hymn. The effect is one not only of gripping intensity, but of a spiritual grandeur rare in the art of our time.

Of the next three symphonies, the Sinfonia Concertante of 1973 for flute, harp, and small string orchestra is more modest in aim, though both its sonorities and its formal design are rich in felicities, and the *Sinfonia Mistica* of 1977 is a work of somewhat withdrawn emotions that yields up its secrets only on long acquaintance. In between, however, Panufnik achieved one of his most challenging and ingenious structures – *Sinfonia di Sfere*, whose unpredictable yet ultimately cogent twists of thought, articulated through skittering string and drum figurations, incisive piano chords, tense woodwind ejaculations, and some weirdly expressive solos for the brass principals, deserve more frequent hearings. On a somewhat smaller scale, the same seems to me to be true of *Metasinfonia* (1978) for solo organ, timpani, and strings, though I know some Panufnik enthusiasts find it one of his less charming works.

Sinfonia Votiva is laid out in two movements, the second a greatly speeded-up recasting of the first. It was written in 1981 for the centenary of the Boston Symphony, and the long, hushed lines of its opening taxed that legendary orchestra's capacities even more arduously than their hectic foreshortenings in the finale. Like *Votiva*, Symphony No. 10, commissioned for the centenary of the Chicago Symphony Orchestra, is a work of characteristic poetry and inwardness. It is interesting to observe how Panufnik's last symphony

– at nineteen minutes, just a little shorter than Lutosławski's – follows a precisely opposite expressive arc, moving from an almost brash assurance in the brass, piano, and percussion fanfares at the start to poignant mystery in the pianissimo harp figure that eventually leaves the music hanging in the air like an enigmatic benison. Meanwhile, in No. 9, Panufnik had created his grandest and most expansive symphony, an absorbing single-movement span whose forty-minute duration ranks it equally with *Arbor Cosmica* (1983) as his longest work.

Arbor Cosmica itself, subtitled '12 Evocations for 12 Strings', is typical Panufnik in a high degree: music of flashing inspiration and deep mystery, whose communicativeness emerges more readily, I feel, than *Sinfonia Mistica*'s from the misleadingly gruff façade of its rigorous triadic construction. The work's unobtrusively masterly writing for strings was emulated six years later, with the addition of eight woodwind instruments, in the gravely beautiful *Harmony* for chamber orchestra, and finds another kind of echo in Panufnik's relatively small but distinguished chamber music output. This includes three string quartets, and an audaciously conceived sextet subtitled 'Train of Thoughts', based on a tiny rhythmic figure that persists unchanged through the work's twelve-minute unfolding, and suggesting the ruminations of a railway traveller. Other instrumental preoccupations yielded four concertos: for piano, violin, bassoon, and cello. These do not constitute a canon to match the scale of the symphonic series, but they are all attractive works, and among their individual movements the Piano Concerto's central Larghetto stands as a ravishing and utterly Panufnikian blend of strict formal unity with simple eloquence.

On the sheer distinctiveness of Panufnik's music it may be useful here to lay some stress, since he has received less general recognition for it than has been accorded to Lutosławski for *his* qualities. Other composers may occasionally come to mind as one considers this or that aspect of Panufnik's style. His penchant for building his pieces out of narrowly restricted sets of notes may remind us of the serialism of Schoenberg and his school, just as his scientific affinities have something in common with Xenakis. The delight in the fundamental materials of music that informs page after page of his work is suggestive of composers as widely different as Bartók and Nielsen. His manner of scoring for clearly separated 'families' of instruments (the woodwind, for instance, set in balanced opposition to the strings) recalls Bruckner; his frequent use of *cantus firmus* as a foundation for proliferating polyphonic lines likewise evokes the methods of Maxwell Davies. Yet Panufnik's music never sounds remotely like that of any of those forerunners or colleagues, for each of these resources and methods is used in an entirely individual way, and in the furtherance of an entirely personal artistic vision.

Interlude

The two composers we have been considering up to this point were born in the second decade of the twentieth century and lived until its tenth. As children, they had to survive the military incursions, boundary shifts, and (for Lutosławski) family uprootings that came with the First World War. Then, being Polish, they were forced as young men and mature adults to undergo not one but two long periods of severe political repression, the first engulfing their country from the west, the second from the east.

It would be idle to speculate on how different the music of Panufnik and Lutosławski might have been without those pressures. But it is at any rate beyond question that Penderecki and Górecki had fewer hurdles to jump in becoming the men and the composers that their mature work shows them to be. For both of them the Second World War was, in all conscience, a gruesome enough environment between the ages of five and eleven, and the Communist takeover likewise had serious consequences when they were in their teens. Yet, by the time they were in their mid-twenties and beginning to make their own mark on Poland's musical life, the long incubus of Nazi and then Stalinist political and ideological tyranny had essentially been lifted, and a new situation faced them and their fellow-artists.

Between 1956 (when Gomułka returned to power) and 1981 (when the Jaruzelski military coup brought martial law), Penderecki and Górecki lived in a country where, despite periods of relative misery on the socio-political front, the arts in general were allowed to flourish with more freedom than at any time since 1939. In music, the Warsaw Autumn Festival had perhaps the highest profile. But beyond that central point of focus, within little more than a decade after the initial thaw, there were as many as nineteen symphony orchestras (not to mention important smaller groups like the Warsaw Chamber Orchestra) operating around Poland. The leading ones often toured abroad, and when they did they usually took Polish works with them.

Many other arts enjoyed a similar pattern of growth. In the visual

Many other arts enjoyed a similar pattern of growth. In the visual field, the gamut stretched from the relatively conservative post-Impressionist 'Colourist' school represented by men like Eugeniusz Eibisch to the bold innovations of Polish poster art. Polish creativity in film embraced the febrile sophistication of Roman Polanski, the satire of Tadeusz Chmielewski, the sensual mysticism of Walerian Borowczyk, and the poetically modulated realism of Jerzy Kawalerowicz, Andrzej Wajda, Andrzej Munk, and their successors.

Above left, a portrait of the artist Eugeniusz Eibisch; *above right*, his *Salvatore* (1919); *opposite, top left*, a poster from Aleksander Ford's film *Knights of the Teutonic Order* (1960); *opposite, top right*, film director Andrzej Wajda, pictured c.1980; *opposite, below*, director Roman Polanski sizes up an angle for his film *Chinatown* (1974).

Scarcely less distinguished rolls could be called in the fields of architecture, poetry, and dramatic production.

For Penderecki and Górecki there were important consequences. In their student days, cultural life was not much different from the way Panufnik and Lutosławski had experienced it in the 1930s, when the world was still open to Polish artists. But whereas, for the senior pair, the doors suddenly closed in their mid-twenties, the generation born in 1933 were greeted at that same age by a new expansion of frontiers. It was around 1960 that these younger men began to be able to travel abroad.

For many of their contemporaries one of the first destinations, naturally enough in the musical climate of the time, was Darmstadt. So it is noteworthy that neither of our two subjects developed any close association with the influential summer courses there – at least, as far as direct participation goes.

Penderecki had only heard such a twentieth-century classic as Stravinsky's *The Rite of Spring* for the first time in 1956 or 1957. Then, in 1958 (as he told Richard Dufallo in an interview published in the book *Trackings*), he made his first acquaintance with some of the latest Western developments when Luigi Nono took some recent scores to Poland. As the Warsaw Autumn gathered impetus, the younger Poles were able to experience Darmstadt as it were on their own home ground.

This meant contact at the same time with the strictly regimented and highly intellectual 'total serialism' of Karlheinz Stockhausen and Pierre Boulez, who sought predetermined rules to control not just pitch but rhythm, dynamics, tone-colour, and articulation as well, and with the very different but equally avant-garde aleatory methods of John Cage. Yet serial techniques and chance elements were to play a relatively restricted part in the development of Penderecki's own polyglot musical language. For himself, he spent only about a week at Darmstadt, and only one of his works – *Emanations*, in 1961 – was premièred there. His own journeys were first of all to Italy (Venice, Florence, Rome, Naples, and Sicily in 1959–60), and then increasingly to such centres as Vienna, Hamburg, Cologne, and Amsterdam. Furthermore, it was with the annual new-music festival in the Black Forest, the Donaueschingen Music Days, rather than with Darmstadt, that his first major artistic alliance was formed.

Górecki, for his part, made his connections with Boulez and Stockhausen in Cologne (where Bruno Maderna, another Darmstadt figure, conducted his *Epitafium* in 1961). He chose Paris for his postgraduate studies, spending three months there in 1961 and returning for a similar period two years later. In his case, the attraction of the French capital was not the great teacher Nadia Boulanger, with whom older Poles like Michał Spisak had gone to study in the 1930s. (Lutosławski had been thinking of doing the same when the onset of war upset his plans; Wojciech Kilar, born in 1932, who was later to compose symphonic poems in a strikingly populist vein, did so now.)

Characteristically, Górecki's view of the contemporary scene centred on a very different kind of musician: Olivier Messiaen, with whose Catholic mysticism, reverence for nature, blend of sensuality and asceticism, preoccupation with rhythm, and taste for extremes in tempo and dynamics he has much in common. Over the years he has come to identify Messiaen as modern music's dominant creator, along with a variety of colleagues who rub shoulders rather surprisingly in his bluntly revisionist lists of modern masters: 'The greatest of the "avant-gardists" in my opinion', he told Norman Lebrecht in a 1990 television interview, 'were Bach, Beethoven, Mozart, Messiaen, Ives'.

Penderecki and Górecki, then, were far from swallowing whole the intoxicating draughts of avant-garde orthodoxy that overwhelmed lesser talents among their compatriots in those heady late-1950s and early-1960s days. Rather, they felt free to pick and choose as their creative needs dictated. With regard to the general tenor of their work, moreover, they were helped by a strictly non-musical circumstance: despite the continuing pressures of Communist (and materialist) ideology in Polish life, the authorities began to realize that a ban on religious subjects could no longer be effectively imposed on artists of their stature.

It is true that a cursory glance at their catalogues might produce a misleading impression. Surprisingly, only about one-fifth of Penderecki's output and a still smaller proportion of Górecki's is explicitly religious in text or subject-matter. But under this heading some of their crucial works, in terms both of inherent quality and of the impact they have made on the public, must be placed. A sense of continuity with Polish and Catholic religious tradition is in any case fundamental to their art and to their lives; so also is their identification with the heritage of Polish folk art, which in any case is

Satire and popular protest
played their part in the
downfall of Polish
Communism: in front of a
giant poster advertising a
Wajda film, Jacek
Federowicz gives a
performance for the crowd
blocking a Warsaw street.

by no means a phenomenon unconnected with religion. In having this avenue of expression reopened to them, they were luckier than the composers who went before them. But this was not all luck, for to a large degree it was the influence of their own work that helped to create the new atmosphere.

4

Penderecki's operatic themes have often been presented in startling visual terms: Satan, in the 1979 Stuttgart production of *Paradise Lost*, watches an Adam and Eve in suitably Edenic costume.

I think I have always written very personal music. I have never concerned myself with what was just fashionable, but composed my own music – even early on, in the avant-garde period. Perhaps that's why the public understood me.

Krzysztof Penderecki, interview with
Kadja Grönke, 1993

Krzysztof Penderecki

By comparison with the reverses and frustrations that have bedevilled many a composer's early life, the course of Krzysztof Penderecki's love for music seems to have run remarkably smooth. The stages of his progress followed each other with an apparent inevitability relatively free of untoward incident.

It is unlikely, of course, that the protagonist would see it that way himself. The person living the life never does. Certainly some of the variegated critical response Penderecki has provoked could be seen from his point of view as untoward. And do not misunderstand: an enormous amount has happened on the way to Penderecki's present eminence. He has written a larger quantity of music than any of the three colleagues he shares this book with (for though there may be more works listed under Lutosławski's name, Penderecki's are written mostly at greater length and often for larger forces). He has also served longer as the head of a music academy, and conducted many more concerts since adding the baton to his professional quiver, than the others' intermittent teaching or performing commitments demanded.

But he has enjoyed more or less uninterrupted success – in the outward sense at least – as a composer, and in becoming one the young Penderecki found few obstacles in his path. To begin with, he had parents who believed in him. His father, Tadeusz, was a lawyer, one of the minority of Polish lawyers to escape extermination by the Nazis; his family came from the Polish Ukraine, and had Lithuanian, Romanian, and Armenian antecedents. Krzysztof's mother, Zofia, came from a Silesian family named Wittgenstein. On both paternal and maternal sides there was interest in the arts, and Tadeusz was a keen enough violinist to play chamber music frequently at home in a variety of informal groups.

Born on 23 November 1933, in the country town of Dębica, east of Kraków, Krzysztof was the second of the couple's three children, three years younger than his brother Janusz, who became a doctor, and seven years older than his sister Barbara. At least one important

Penderecki in 1975 with his father Tadeusz

element in the artist he later became was determined during the war years, while he was still a child: an enduring concern with the subjects of freedom and oppression. He has spoken of the horror he felt watching the rounding up of Jews in the streets. On one occasion, he was caught writing anti-Nazi slogans on the lavatory walls at school. Tadeusz, who had to defend his son against threatened expulsion, told this story to Wolfram Schwinger, the German musicologist, for years director of the Stuttgart Opera, who has written a substantial book about the composer.

Zofia Penderecka is said to have had priestly ambitions for her son, but his father envisaged an artistic future for him from early on. At first the taste for sculpture and painting predominated. Penderecki has a penchant for things visual, and still enjoys collecting icons, portraits, and handsome pieces of furniture. Like his fascination with magic, superstition, the weirder manifestations of religious belief, and the more out-of-the-way sciences, this field of interest has had its effect on the mature composer's choice of subjects, especially when he came to write operas. Music, however, soon took first place among his enthusiasms. Along with his other lessons at the Dębica *gimnazjum,* he studied the violin with Stanisław Darłak, who taught at the school and also conducted the town's military band.

The sight of Jews being rounded up by German soldiers in the Warsaw of his childhood was an early factor in focusing Penderecki's attention on the subject of oppression, treated in many of his works.

Darłak seems to have been an effective and inspiring teacher. By the time Krzysztof was fourteen, he was good enough to play a Vivaldi concerto in public. For a time he actually considered a career as a virtuoso violinist. (Shocking though they seemed by conventional standards, the new playing techniques he was to demand in his string-orchestral works of the late 1950s and early 1960s stemmed from an intimate knowledge of the violin family's potential and character.) Then, when he passed his school-leaving exams at the age of seventeen, he went off to Kraków to continue his musical education while also studying philosophy, Greek, and Latin as an extramural student at the city's famous Jagellonian University (one of the oldest in the world, founded in 1364). He now took violin lessons privately with Stanisław Tawroszewicz, and studied theory with Franciszek Skołyszewski (a former piano pupil of Egon Petri), to such effect that he completed five years of intermediate music schoolwork in two years.

The renowned Jagellonian University in Kraków, which in 1911 had hosted the first seminar in Poland on music history

From 1954 to 1958 Penderecki studied at the Kraków Academy of Music. After the first of those four years (at just two years older than Lutosławski had been when he made a similar decision) he dropped his violin studies to concentrate exclusively on composition.

Penderecki's first teacher at the Academy was Artur Malawski, a highly regarded composer who, like Panufnik, had studied under Kazimierz Sikorski in Warsaw. When Malawski died in 1957 at the age of fifty-three, Penderecki officially joined Stanisław Wiechowicz's composition class, though he admitted later to Schwinger that most of his work in preparing for final exams the following year was done on his own.

Graduating from the Academy in 1958 with the highest distinction, Penderecki was immediately invited to teach composition there himself. At a theological college in the city, he also gave a course in Renaissance Polish church music (some of which he was later to conduct, and to draw upon in his own religious works), and he did some writing for the journal *Ruch Muzyczne* ('Musical Movement').

Penderecki in 1958, the year of his graduation from the Kraków Academy of Music

Penderecki's own output, juvenilia apart, had begun with a violin sonata written in 1953; after setting it aside for years, he was eventually to revive it for performance and publication in 1990. Student works subsequently withdrawn included two songs written in 1955 and 1958 and a string quartet dating from 1956–7. By contrast, a set of Three Miniatures for clarinet and piano was later published. There was also a more ambitious composition: the *Epitafium* in memory of Artur Malawski, for string orchestra and timpani, which gave the 24-year-old composer his first real taste of orchestral performance when the Kraków Philharmonic under Michał Baranowski played it in June 1958 as his graduation exercise. Within its basically elegiac frame, critics have found hints in *Epitafium* of the explosive quality that was to emerge in later Penderecki works.

But the real breakthrough was to come remarkably soon. For the second competition for young composers organized in 1959 by the League of Polish Composers, Penderecki decided to enter his three latest works: *From the Psalms of David*, a piece for mixed chorus and instruments from 1958, *Emanations* for two string orchestras begun then and finished in 1959, and – the most recent piece – *Strophes* for soprano, speaker, and ten instruments. As with most competitions of its kind, submissions had to be anonymous. So the judges (who included Lutosławski, Sikorski, and Wiechowicz) must have been as surprised as everyone else, including the composer, when the three prizewinning works turned out to have all been written by Penderecki.

Rather like those wonderful Prix de Rome that launched so many French composers on their travels in the nineteenth century (and so many American ones on theirs in the twentieth), Penderecki's spoils in this first competitive success included money to pay for a two-month visit to Italy, on which he set off before the end of the year. But meanwhile, in September, both *From the Psalms of David* and *Strophes* had been performed. *Psalms* was given in Kraków by the Philharmonic Chorus and Orchestra, and *Strophes* by the chamber orchestra of the Silesian Philharmonic at the Warsaw Autumn Festival, with the influential conductor-composer Andrzej Markowski on the podium on both occasions.

Thus, by the time he reached his twenty-sixth birthday, most of the pointers to a major career for Penderecki were already in evidence, and so were some central elements of an individual musical language. These stylistic traits will be set in context in Chapter 6. As for the impact the music made, my own review of a Chicago performance of the *Psalms of David* in 1968 was fairly typical of critical response at large:

> *It is not only an early work but also, clearly, a work written in a country intoxicated by the flood of cultural influences consequent on the liberalization of 1956. I thought it rather wicked programming to juxtapose the piece with Stravinsky's 1930 Symphony of Psalms, for much of Penderecki's obsessive, chant-like choral writing is directly descended from that classic.*

> *However, if this fifteen-minute composition is unabashedly derivative, the fact is itself characteristic of the cheerful eclecticism to be found equally in Penderecki's later, more fully achieved work. The dark, shadowy wailings of its quieter sections are more original and no less prophetic.*

In the light of his own statement, some years afterwards, 'I take what I can use and make something new out of it', I see no need to apologize a quarter of a century later for the phrase 'cheerful eclecticism'; and the prophetic quality of the 'dark, shadowy wailings' has surely been borne out in a long line of works, orchestral as well as vocal, from the *Threnody* for strings by way of the *St Luke Passion* to the *Polish Requiem* and beyond.

One of the crucial factors that led Penderecki to fame and fortune turned out tò be *Strophes*. Through this little piece, barely seven minutes long, he not only gained an admirer in Pierre Boulez (who programmed it in his Paris *Domaine Musical* series); he also acquired both a publisher for the next nine years (Hermann Moeck, from Celle in Germany, who heard the Warsaw performance of *Strophes*) and a highly fruitful association with the Donaueschingen Music Days (to whose guiding spirit, Heinrich Strobel, Moeck enthusiastically brought a tape from the Polish Radio broadcast).

Strobel, a former critic, was also director of the music division of the Southwest German Radio in Baden-Baden, and immediately commissioned a piece from Penderecki for the 1960 Donaueschingen Festival. Titled *Anaklasis* ('Refraction of Light'), and scored for forty-two string instruments and percussion, it was sketched towards the end of 1959, completed in Italy between December and February, and first performed on 16 October 1960 under the direction of the Baden-Baden orchestra's great Austrian-born conductor, Hans Rosbaud.

The audience's reaction to the flashing sonorities of *Anaklasis* – an ovation that demanded an encore – was perhaps the first major clue to Penderecki's exceptional power of communication. New music tends more often to garner boos or catcalls than encores, and even in the somewhat esoteric environment of specialist contemporary-music festivals such a triumph is a rarity. Yet it happened with the dramatic, starkly gestural *Anaklasis*; I recall the sense of occasion in the Amsterdam Concertgebouw when it happened with the *Threnody* for strings at the 1963 ISCM Festival; and it happened again in 1964 at the première of the Sonata for Cello and Orchestra (after *Anaklasis* and the 1961–2 *Fluorescences*, Penderecki's third Donaueschingen/Southwest German Radio commission).

With the addition of the Capriccio for violin and orchestra in 1967 and *Actions* for jazz ensemble in 1971, the number of Penderecki's Donaueschingen commissions reached five. By this time, from the springboard Heinrich Strobel had offered him, the composer's fame had travelled far beyond the sleepy little German country town. His style had moved in radically different directions, exemplified in the new monumentality and religious fervour of the *St Luke Passion* and

Utrenja. These works, and the 1960 *Threnody* with its revolutionary notation based on measured seconds instead of periodic beats, had won him celebrity in the United States as well.

There were big changes in Penderecki's personal life during this period too. His first marriage, to Barbara, a pianist, who in 1955 bore him a daughter named Beata, had not lasted long. (It seems somehow characteristic of his ability to reinvent himself that this episode in his life is little chronicled, even in Schwinger's extensive biography.) In December 1965, in Dębica, Penderecki married his second wife, Elżbieta Solecka, whose father was principal cellist of the Kraków Philharmonic Orchestra. The couple were to take a small flat in Dębica – later they moved to Kraków – but before this they went off to the winter resort of Krynica in the mountains near Zakopane, which was for years one of Penderecki's favourite spots for relaxed composition. In 1966, after the première of the *St Luke Passion* in Münster Cathedral, the province of North Rhine/Westphalia awarded Penderecki its Great Prize for Art. An invitation to teach composition at the Folkwang Academy in Essen followed, the Polish government sanctioned the move, and a complicated time of multi-national residences began for the Pendereckis, whose son Łukasz had been born on 7 April.

During the winter of 1967–8, encouraged by increasing success, they bought a plot of land in the peaceful Kraków suburb of Wola

Penderecki with his second wife Elżbieta in the late 1960s

The Pendereckis in 1979
with their children Łukasz
and Dominika

Justowska, where they would build their first real house. While it was
being made ready, there were two more moves. In September 1968,
invited to be guests for two years by the German Academic Exchange
Service, Penderecki and his wife took a flat in the Zehlendorf area of
West Berlin, where he had the status of an official resident composer.
He was soon in demand in Vienna as well, where the Austrian Radio
invited him to spend a period as adviser to its music department. His
residence there, interrupted by constant travelling, ran for a year from
November 1970 (during which time, on 16 March 1971, the second of
Following page, for many   the Penderecki's two children, their daughter Dominika, was born). A
winters, the Tatra mountains   few weeks after returning to Kraków, in the middle of December 1971,
offered Penderecki a peaceful they were finally able to move into the house in Wola Justowska,
setting for composition away
from city stress.   which had taken four years to build.

Penderecki's reputation was spreading on both sides of the Atlantic. He had visited the United States for the first time in November 1967 for the American première of the *St Luke Passion* in Minneapolis. Intensified by the American première of his first opera, *The Devils of Loudun,* at Santa Fe in 1969, his triumphal progress reached a peak when the United Nations commissioned the work – *Cosmogony* – that would celebrate its twenty-fifth anniversary in October 1970. A few weeks before that, Eugene Ormandy had given the US première of *Utrenja I* in Philadelphia and recorded it. Penderecki was becoming a familiar participant in competition juries – Gaudeamus in Holland in 1967, and the Marie José Competition in Switzerland in 1968, were just two of these. He received the Sibelius Gold Medal in London in December 1967, started work on the music for Alain Resnais's film *Je t'aime, je t'aime* in Paris the following month, and went on from there to Berlin to hear Herbert von Karajan conduct *Polymorphia.* Such widespread dissemination of his music was by now making it hard for his publisher, the small house of Moeck, to keep up with the demand for performing materials. In 1968 therefore, with personal regret but bowing to professional realities, he signed an agreement with B. Schott's Söhne of Mainz, which had started its activities in the year of Beethoven's birth, and was henceforth to be Penderecki's exclusive publisher.

The change was prompted in particular by the complex needs of opera production, for it was at this time that the theatre came to take a dominant place in Penderecki's scheme of work. From now on he was to work as much with poets, stage directors, and scenic artists as with his fellow-musicians. For *The Devils of Loudun,* based on John Whiting's dramatization of the Aldous Huxley novel, Penderecki wrote his own libretto, using a translation by one of the leading poets of twentieth-century Germany, Erich Fried. The visual aspects of the original 1969 Hamburg production by Konrad Swinarski, with sets by Lidia and Jerzy Skarżyński, drew considerable criticism. But just two days later Stuttgart mounted the opera, and the presence of Günther Rennert as director and Leni Bauer-Ecsy as set designer established a pattern of high-level theatrical collaboration that was henceforth to be the norm for Penderecki.

Rennert's contribution to *The Devils* prompted a rapid reassessment of a work that had simply bored a large proportion of its

Opposite, the electrifying 1969 Stuttgart production of The Devils of Loudun swiftly vindicated a work that had fallen relatively flat at its Hamburg première.

Hamburg audience. This time the public was electrified by a
production that, in Wolfram Schwinger's words, 'did not so much
narrate as hurl the spectator into the drama of the events'. Where
Swinarski had seemed to pull his punches, Rennert took the veils
(such as the tapestry drop that softened the impact of the execution
scene in Hamburg) off the action, and the clothes off several of the
characters. In a long review in the *Frankfurter allgemeine Zeitung*
headlined 'Revision by Production', Klaus Wagner observed:

> *Rennert takes naturalism that much further, making Swinarski's show
> of realism cringe like a modest stage-designer's first maquette, and to a
> point where the art of stage illusion is turned into critical irony.*

When Swinarski staged *The Devils* in Santa Fe, he had the
advantage of Rouben Ter-Arutunian's striking designs, and his own
directorial work thus came across more strongly than it had in

Masks were a prominent
feature in Penderecki's third
and fourth operas. Harry
Kupfer directed the 1986
Salzburg Festival première
of *The Black Mask*, above –
behind the mask is the
soprano Josephine Barstow.

August Everding was
responsible for the première
of *Ubu Rex* in Munich five
years later, *right*.

Hamburg. Penderecki's subsequent operatic ventures have involved such leading directors as August Everding, who was responsible for both the 1979 Stuttgart production of *Paradise Lost* and the 1991 première of *Ubu Rex* at the Bavarian State Opera in Munich, and Harry Kupfer, who collaborated with the composer on the libretto of *The Black Mask* and directed its première at the 1986 Salzburg Festival.

Nor was the participation of Kupfer the only controversial element in Penderecki's developing operatic career. It was for purely practical reasons that Virginio Puecher initially replaced Sam Wanamaker as director of *Paradise Lost*, commissioned for the 1976 US Bicentennial by Lyric Opera of Chicago, and eventually, after delays in the composition, first performed there in November 1978. But Puecher himself became embroiled in the sort of artistic dispute that had dogged his work elsewhere. He resigned 'after differences of opinion with the composer', whereupon Igal Perry, a young Israeli associated with the choreography of the production from the start, bravely took over directorial responsibility. In his penchant for last-minute deliveries of scores, moreover, Penderecki showed himself a true theatre man in the Rossini tradition – at rehearsals for the première of *The Black Mask*, Schwinger relates, 'the Vienna Philharmonic Orchestra and the conductor Woldemar Nelsson found the ink still wet on the pages set before them'.

No doubt inevitably, as Penderecki became increasingly preoccupied with traditional genres, the chorus of acclaim that had at first greeted his music began to be variegated with more than a few discordant voices of complaint. The criticism, when it came, was from both sides of the stylistic divide.

Some of the gibes directed from the traditionalist ranks at the modernist aspect of Penderecki were mild enough. When Frank Howes wrote about the *Threnody* in *The Times* of London after that vociferously cheered Amsterdam performance in 1963, he remarked mischievously that the composer had called on his string players to do everything with their instruments 'short of actually playing them'. For Penderecki himself, as Schwinger noted, 'sound includes noise'. It was his 'refusal to admit a difference between the two' that led him to develop a whole sophisticated new range of hitting, tapping, scraping, sliding, and violent plucking effects in his string writing around 1960.

In some of the works of this period, however, a tell-tale new device

Originally conceived in the
1890s, Alfred Jarry's
burlesque satire *Ubu roi*
took on vivid new relevance
in the cultural climate of
Penderecki's operatic
treatment a century later.
This scene is from the
Munich première in 1991.

began to appear. Another string piece, *Polymorphia*, written in 1961, concerns itself almost throughout with further extensions of the *Threnody*'s noise techniques. But at the end the polymorphic din is resolved with a sudden, unexpected, sumptuous, and 'beautiful' C major chord played with unimpeachably 'normal' technique by the whole string orchestra.

When the piece was first performed in Hamburg in April 1962, one reviewer suggested that it 'would have provoked unhesitating protest if the composer had not resorted to a glorious, old-fashioned common chord for his final full stop'. The correspondent of the *Hamburger Abendblatt* and his colleagues did not realize it at the time, but that one innocent – or perhaps not so innocent – chord carried the seed of a mighty *volte-face*. It constituted the first tiny step in a progression that was soon to land Penderecki in a completely different set of black books.

Two years later, in the *Stabat Mater*, he took up once again the idea of ending with an exultant major chord, this time after a mostly hushed and lugubriously chromatic piece. When the *Stabat Mater* was itself included in the *St Luke Passion*, its own major chord was matched by another one at the end of the whole work – the chords had now, by the way, moved methodically upwards from C through D to E major – and a further range of traditional references, including most notably the use of Gregorian chant, was pressed into service in the construction of a musical edifice of monumental scale and powerfully nineteenth-century gesture.

For some critics, as for the vast majority of the audiences that encountered this landmark piece, the *St Luke Passion* counted 'among the most significant compositions in our new music', or (in the words of the veteran Hans Heinz Stuckenschmidt) joined the religious works of Webern and Stravinsky as 'the most important bridge between the spirit of the liturgy and modern music'. Yet, whereas traditionally minded critics like the *Süddeutsche Zeitung*'s Joachim Kaiser concluded that 'the richness of perspective, high stature, artistic eloquence, visionary strength, and theological completeness of Bach's *St Matthew Passion* are not to be mentioned in the same breath as Penderecki's dissonances', it was precisely his consonances that were beginning to get him into trouble with the modernists.

Opposite, Jerzy Katlewicz conducting Penderecki's *St Luke Passion* in June 1980, in the sumptuous baroque setting of St Bernard's Church, Kraków

The trouble with eclecticism, as far as critical judgement is concerned, is how easy it makes it for an artist to attract condemnation from the parties on both sides. For the public – now, increasingly, general audiences and not just the new-music-festival crowd – the Penderecki of works like *Anaklasis* and the *Threnody* represented the acceptable face of modernism. With its uncompromising emotional directness, the *Threnody* in particular had already established itself around the world as a kind of avant-garde calling card, and the additional attraction of the *St Luke Passion*'s links with religious and musical tradition cemented Penderecki's status as a bold yet approachable synthesist. But in the press, depending on the individual writer's standpoint, he was in danger of being seen either as a Philistine whose crude aesthetic of noise – *'bruitisme'* – disqualified him from inclusion in the pantheon, or as an opportunist who had 'betrayed' the sacred esoteric values of the avant-garde for the sake of popular success. Either way, the *St Luke Passion* was a watershed for its composer, who was henceforth regarded by critics and public alike in a new light.

Penderecki's initial sortie into the operatic world with *The Devils of Loudun* in 1969 was followed by the appearance of further retrospective-sounding religious works like the two parts of *Utrenja* in 1970 and 1971, and by his first trafficking in the highly un-avant-garde genre of the symphony in 1973. In the latter case, a traditional conception was fused with elements of the sound-world he had established in earlier, more exploratory pieces. The backlash from the modernist camp intensified to outright contempt in the later 1970s with the appearance of two of Penderecki's most 'reactionary' or 'opportunistic' works, which not only showed a realignment with traditional forms, but also largely abandoned his beach-heads in the realm of new sounds and innovative notation in favour of more familiar sonorities and conventional methods of indicating the passage of music through time. The works in question were the Violin Concerto, premièred in Basle in 1977 (and not by anyone with the new-music world's stamp of approval but, if you please, by that denizen of the traditional concert and recital platform Isaac Stern), and the fundamentally tonal, consonant, and dramatically and musically leisurely 'sacra rappresentazione' *Paradise Lost*. (Whatever the critics said, one of the proudest moments of all, for a Polish Catholic, must have been the special concert performance of the

Assisted by the composer, Isaac Stern (centre) and Moshe Atzmon (right) prepare for the 1977 première of Penderecki's Violin Concerto in Basle.

second act of *Paradise Lost* that the La Scala company, collaborators with Lyric Opera on the work's first production, gave for Pope John Paul II in the Vatican shortly after presenting the work's European première in January 1979.)

For the composer himself neither subjects nor styles presented any problem. As for subject, he had told me in an interview in Minneapolis in 1967, when I commented on the emergence of the *St Luke Passion* in a secular society like 'People's Poland',

> *Well, I am a Catholic, but membership in a given church is not really the point. It's rather that I am very much concerned with these topics – Auschwitz, Hiroshima in my* Threnody, *and the implications of the Passion, which after all is still one of the most topical, and indeed universal, stories. And I am concerned with these things in an essentially moral and social way, not in either a political or a sectarian religious way.*

Asked whether there was any official discouragement of religious expression in music, he went on:

> *Oh, no, absolutely not. I must state this quite clearly. We write what we want to write, without any restrictions or directives at all. And when we have written it, the state helps us in every possible way, with publications, performances, and so on.*

Chicago's Lyric Opera gave
the world première of
Penderecki's *Paradise Lost*
in 1978; Dennis Wayne and
Nancy Thuesen are pictured
dancing the parts of Adam
and Eve; in the background
are their vocal counterparts,
sung by William Stone and
Ellen Shade.

In this broadly favourable climate, Penderecki quite naturally went on cultivating his affinity for grand sacred subjects, following *Utrenja* with such works as *Canticum Canticorum Salomonis* in 1970–73, the Magnificat a year later, the Te Deum in 1979–80, and above all the vast and compendious *Polish Requiem* completed in 1984. The line of operas that already contained *The Devils of Loudun* and *Paradise Lost* was extended too, with *The Black Mask* in 1984–6 and *Ubu Rex* in 1990–91. In all these works, Penderecki's fundamental predilection for stark juxtapositions – of massed sound-clusters with etiolated single lines, of shimmering whisper with violent ejaculation – found an apt dramatic habitat.

Opposite, the advent of Lech Wałesa and Pope John Paul II as political and spiritual leaders created a new context for religious music in Poland.

The declaration of martial law in December 1981, which Penderecki heard about while on a visit to Frankfurt, left him momentarily wondering what the future held for him in Poland, but he was soon assured that he would still be granted visas for foreign travel, and he was back in Kraków by the end of January 1982. The following year, when the German newspaper *Die Welt* attacked him for implicitly supporting the Jaruzelski government by accepting a state honour, he replied:

I express myself through my sacred music, which I have been composing for twenty-five years in this Communist country. My position must be clear, yet the government has honoured my fiftieth birthday, and I can only be thankful that an artist has been honoured in spite of ideological differences of opinion.

In the sphere of musical language itself, Penderecki also went on writing what he wanted to write, and concentrating on his central aim of communicating with as broad a public as possible. The accession of a Polish Pope was certainly one element that strengthened his position when he chose religious subjects. But he also played a role in secular events without making any ideological separation between sacred and profane: commissioned by Lech Wałesa's Solidarity union in 1980 to write a piece for the unveiling of a memorial to the Gdańsk dockworkers killed in the uprising ten years earlier, he responded with the *Lacrimosa* for soprano, chorus, and orchestra, which in due course became part of the *Polish Requiem.* The critical salvos have continued – always offset by a no less extreme enthusiasm in other quarters – but

they seem to have had little or no effect on Penderecki's career.

From 1971 on, it would be more accurate to speak of 'careers'. It was in that year that Penderecki made his public conducting début, with the première of his latest Donaueschingen commission, the jazz-ensemble piece *Actions*. Leading the specially assembled International Free Jazz Orchestra on this occasion, he cut (as Schwinger puts it) 'a thoroughly presentable figure as a conductor'. Ever since his youthful violinist days, Penderecki had enjoyed being in direct physical contact with music. One of the first musical fruits of the mid-1950s cultural thaw had been the setting up of Polish Radio's experimental electronic studio in Warsaw. Penderecki had often worked there on his film or incidental-music projects, and on other pieces such as the electronic *Psalmus* in 1961. Another product of these activities – an electronically manipulated vocal Hymn for the opening of the Munich Olympic Games – was to follow in 1971. But with the success of his conducting venture on the friendly ground of Donaueschingen, he began to find the experience of direct collaboration with players and singers irresistible.

Within a year or two, not surprisingly, Penderecki had become one of the principal exponents of his own works, recording many of them himself. Beginning in 1973 (with Stravinsky's *Firebird* Suite) he added the music of other composers to his programmes. Shostakovich's Fifth and Fourteenth Symphonies became particular favourites, as did various pieces by Stravinsky and Sibelius. For several years he has worked on a regular basis with the Kraków Philharmonic, programming and conducting music from all segments of the repertoire, and as Principal Guest Conductor of the North German Radio (NDR) Symphony Orchestra in Hamburg. In yet another stylistic context, the 1982 International Organ Week in Nuremberg gave him the chance to indulge one of his earliest enthusiasms: here, he juxtaposed vocal compositions by some of the greatest Polish Renaissance masters with his own choral pieces.

None of this varied activity stemmed the flow of new Penderecki compositions. The symphonic trend in particular continued with a steadily expanding series of works. The Second (*Christmas*) Symphony was first performed by Zubin Mehta and the New York Philharmonic in May 1980. At the 1988 Lucerne Festival Penderecki himself gave the première of a large-scale orchestral Passacaglia; standing alone on that occasion, it is eventually to be part of a Third Symphony, scheduled for performance by the Munich Philharmonic in December 1995, but still uncompleted at the time of writing. It has meanwhile been overtaken by two further symphonies. No. 4, which started life as an even more massive orchestral Adagio over half an hour in duration, commissioned to mark the bicentenary of the *Declaration des Droits de l'Homme et du Citoyen*, was first conducted by Lorin Maazel with the Orchestre National de France in Paris in November 1989. No. 5,

Penderecki conducted his own and other composers' music with growing success from 1971.

Penderecki's Second Cello
Concerto had its première
in Berlin in 1983: Mstislav
Rostropovich, for whom so
many twentieth-century cello
concertos have been
composed, was the soloist.

commissioned by the International Cultural Society of Korea, was first performed by the Seoul Philharmonic Orchestra under the composer's direction in August 1992.

Penderecki's relatively small catalogue of chamber music, too, was expanded with the completion of a String Trio in 1991 and a Quartet for clarinet and string trio two years later. Commissioned respectively by the Baden-Württemberg Ministry of Culture and the Schleswig-Holstein Music Festival, the two works were subsequently arranged as Sinfonietta No. 1 for strings and Sinfonietta No. 2 for clarinet and strings.

As if all this were not enough, a third career had been inaugurated in 1972: Penderecki accepted the post of Principal at the Kraków Academy of Music, where he had himself studied and where he had done his first teaching. It is probably true to say that his workload during the years he held the position was light, partly because he sensibly contrived to exert his influence through the appointment of trusted former pupils like Krzysztof Meyer and Marek Stachowski in adjutant positions, but he took and has continued to take a keen interest in the welfare of his old school. In 1973 he also accepted a professorship at Yale University in New Haven, Connecticut, where he bought a house for use during his family's extended stays there over the next few years, and in 1975 he gave some lectures at the Florida State University School of Music in Tallahassee.

Unless we were to devote a few hundred pages to it, listing of the places where Penderecki has conducted, or the distinctions that have come his way, would be impossible. How exhausting it must have been for the man himself can only be conjectured – by comparison, even Lutosławski at his busiest looks like a stay-at-home. To give the merest idea of what Penderecki's schedule is like, one entirely typical year will serve: in 1983, he travelled to – and in most cases conducted in – Berlin, Breda, Tilburg, 's-Hertogenbosch, Eindhoven, Paris, Vienna, Moscow, Leningrad, Dresden, Florence, New York, New Haven, London, Lyon, Rome, Venice, Helsinki, London again, Hanover, Melbourne, Brisbane, Sydney, Berlin again, Washington, and Rome again.

Starting with a doctorate from the Eastman School of Music at the University of Rochester in New York State conferred in 1972, Penderecki has received honorary degrees from universities on both sides of the Atlantic. He holds honorary memberships or fellowships of musical academies in London, Rome, Stockholm, Berlin, and Buenos Aires, and has been honoured by the governments of Germany, France, and the Principality of Monaco.

In 1980 the Polish Radio devoted a festival to Penderecki's music in Kraków, his home base since student days. The most impressive of his many prizes for composition came with the bestowing of the University of Louisville's Grawemeyer Award for the Adagio (Symphony No. 4) in 1992. That combination of foreign successes and domestic links has been characteristic of his career all along.

Apart from some patches of ill health suffered by Elżbieta, Penderecki's family life has provided an essential core of stability in this whirlwind of activity. The house at Wola Justowska is one peaceful place conducive to creative thought, and years of winter visits to Krynica have provided the refreshment of variety. Since 1980 the family has rented another property: a country estate at Lusławice, fifty miles from Kraków. The restoration and decoration of the eighteenth-century buildings have given Penderecki a new field of

The eighteenth-century country house at Lusławice, stylishly restored by Penderecki, and the scene of several chamber-music festivals since 1980

activity for his visual sense, and he has organized several chamber music festivals there for invited guests. The most recent residential development has been the acquisition of a flat in Lucerne, where the Pendereckis spend what free time they can find.

By the end of 1994, the number of Penderecki's compositions had mounted to seventy-five. What is surprising is perhaps not that he has written so much music, but that he has managed to write music at all. The labour has been Herculean. We shall consider in Chapter 6 what it has produced.

5

Górecki talks about music –
characteristically, with
books about Bach and
Beethoven at his elbow.

*Why do I write music? I've done it all my life,
since I was little – I can't do otherwise. I need it.
But I don't know why. I hear something. There's
always something sounding in my head ... It's
old-fashioned, maybe. Science, construction –
that's done in my workroom, it doesn't come
outside. Making combinations, high technique
– that disappears in the music. You hear only
music. Where does the secret lie?*

Henryk Mikołaj Górecki, in a Dutch
television interview, 1993

Henryk Górecki

Each of the four Poles considered in this book stands apart, both from the other three and from his background, in a way distinctly his own. Panufnik was the only one to cut his ties with his country, going into self-imposed exile at the age of thirty-nine. Penderecki has written four operas, thus devoting a sizeable proportion of his creative effort to a genre that attracted the other three in varying degrees but that they eventually avoided. It is not just a questionably clever joke to suggest that, for Lutosławski, not being an odd man out was precisely his way of being the odd man out: whatever political or aesthetic compromises his three colleagues may at one time or another have been forced to make, Lutosławski was much more a master of keeping his individuality under wraps, of finding ways of coexisting with pernicious regimes while somehow maintaining an area of inner artistic validity.

Górecki, for his part, has stayed close to his roots, largely undistracted by the public round of activities as performer, competition judge, administrator, and festival attender that has to a greater or lesser extent distracted the other three from the laborious, intellectually demanding, emotionally draining, and ultimately private business of actually writing music. While his colleagues were fulfilling, with individually varying degrees of reluctance or enthusiasm, the requirements placed on them by government fiat or performing schedule or administrative responsibility, Górecki was the one that stayed at home. He did accept the post of Principal at the State Academy of Music in Katowice in 1975; but this activity was cut short only four years later when he resigned. Even Panufnik, certainly a no less private man at heart, did not succeed until his fiftieth year in achieving the quiet and settled mode of life, so helpful to creative thought, that has been the rule for Górecki since his youth.

From this it follows among other things that a chronicle of Górecki's life and career is much less eventful than is the case with any of his three colleagues. He has not built up a performing career,

David Drew, pictured
here with Górecki, has
played a vital role as
a music publisher of flair
and discernment.

travelled the festival circuit, or involved himself in contemporary
music organizations or competitions. As he put it a few years ago in a
long Press discussion chaired by David Drew (formerly Director of
Publications at Górecki's publisher, Boosey & Hawkes):

> *I'm not a globetrotter. Where did Beethoven go? Just to Heiligenstadt –*
> *that's a good model for me.*

That interview and other rare exceptions aside, Górecki has
persistently resisted such forms of promotion, on the principle that
composition – and life itself – are personal activities in which a man
has his right to privacy. In any case, he says:

> *I don't like journalists. I like to talk at length. When I talk to*
> *journalists, the strange things I say are taken out of context, and then*
> *they're even stranger, even sillier.*

There is a moral element in Górecki's stance: 'I hate commerce in
music', he has said – 'I am not interested in career'. An innate
tendency towards this sort of self-effacement has undoubtedly been
reinforced by recurring bouts of poor health, including serious
illnesses in 1973 and again eleven years later.

For someone uninterested 'in career', what has happened to Górecki in the 1990s can only be accounted astonishing, and more than a little ironic. Seemingly at a stroke, this obscure Pole transformed the shape of the so-called music business (a phrase he would undoubtedly detest), attracting to the long-isolated world of 'serious' new music the kind of mass and media attention formerly associated only with such phenomena as Elvis Presley and the Beatles, and establishing himself as one of the most widely known, admired, and listened-to composers in the history of the art. Not even Penderecki, with the epiphany of the *Threnody* and the *St Luke Passion* thirty years earlier, had broken so decisively through the sound-barrier into the consciousness of the broad public.

The piece with which Górecki effected this metamorphosis was not even new. For many years, since first becoming a professional musician in the second half of the 1950s, he has had his successes, but was little known beyond the ranks of new-music specialists, and his reputation outside Poland was minor in comparison with Panufnik's, Lutosławski's, or Penderecki's. Then, in 1992, a recording of his Third Symphony, composed as far back as 1976, suddenly appeared on the best-seller lists in Britain, the United States, and several other countries, and, having appeared there, stayed for months on end, selling over 300,000 copies by the middle of 1993. That figure, moreover, had passed the 1,000,000 mark at the time of writing (mid 1995).

As it is inclined to do on such occasions, the world asked some cynical questions. They were the same questions as had been asked about Penderecki when he made a similar transition in the 1960s and 70s, 'pandering to the low taste of his audience and seeking easy successes by discarding new compositional techniques', as one critic, Grzegorz Michałski, put it. Górecki too had been in the forefront of modernist developments at the start of his career. Did not his conversion now to extreme simplicity and untrammelled emotional directness betoken a comparable sell-out? Was the public acclaim it gained for him a mere, cheaply-bought seven-day wonder? I think anyone who takes a look at his character, as far as an outsider can read such things, and who considers the way he has lived his life, will find it hard to reach a cynical conclusion. For everything about Górecki's personality, his music, and his way of talking about music proclaims a man as solid and single-minded (or single-soul'd) all the way through as Panufnik was.

The milieu that produced Górecki was a humbler, earthier one than the family backgrounds of his colleagues in this book. His parents, according to someone who knows him well, were 'simple village people'. The English word 'peasant' is a dangerous one to use, for peasantry is not a surviving phenomenon in twentieth-century England, but in continental Europe the notion of a peasant class with rural roots, integrity, traditional religious beliefs, and often at the same time high intellectual standards and a lively regard for the arts has not lost its currency. It is this kind of background that Górecki's music, his statements about music, and his physical presence – the very voice and figure of the man – all proclaim.

In continental Europe, the peasant environment that nurtured Górecki's personality and music continues to flourish in country and town alike.

Henryk Mikołaj Górecki was born on 6 December 1933 in the village of Czernica, near Rybnik in the Silesian coal-mining area, close to the Czech border. There was no musical activity to speak of in Czernica, though the young Górecki was able to hear a few performances in Rybnik. Not surprisingly, then, serious thought of a musical career began much later with him than with many composers, and on leaving school in 1951 he taught for two years in a primary school before starting to study music intensively. His studies actually began in 1952 while he was still a teacher. The following year he left

Even against the soulless architectural background of modern industrial Katowice, people still gather together convivially in the old way.

Górecki at the 1966
Warsaw Autumn Festival
with Bolesław Szabelski,
the former Szymanowski
pupil who had been
Górecki's composition
teacher at the Katowice
State Academy of Music

his job to concentrate on music, and in 1955, after three years at the
Intermediate School of Music in Rybnik, he enrolled at the State
Academy of Music in Katowice (his home city since then), studying
composition for the next five years with the former Szymanowski
pupil Bolesław Szabelski. In 1959, a year before graduating with
first-class honours, he married Jadwiga Rurańska, a piano teacher,
and the couple were later to be colleagues on the teaching staff of
the Academy.

Summarized thus, Górecki's early career looks uneventful
enough, but the narrative conceals two enormous dramas: the
beginnings of his long history of illness, and the war. He does not
talk much about his family's sufferings during the Nazi period,
though the camps claimed victims among his relatives. What
emerges, from such reminiscences as were contained in a television
feature about Górecki broadcast on the BBC's South Bank Show
and directed by Tony Palmer, is the long view he takes of such
matters. The images he retains of the period, even in restrospect, are
immediate enough:

> *I remember, when I was twelve years old, we went on a school visit to*
> *Auschwitz. I had the feeling that the huts were still warm … The paths*
> *themselves – and this image has never left me – the paths were made from*

The concentration camp at Auschwitz, where Górecki remembers 'walking on human beings' as a twelve-year-old on a school visit. 'Work makes you free,' proclaims the chilling inscription over the gates.

*human bones, thrown onto the path like shingle. We boys – how to walk
on this? This is not sand, not earth. We were walking on human beings.*

But as man and artist Górecki sees these things as part of a process
that is sadly far from being over:

*This was my world. The only way to confront this horror, to forget –
but you could never forget – was through music ... The world today, it's
the same. Also a nightmare, crushing us. Somehow I had to take a stand,
as a witness, and as a warning ... The war, the rotten times under
Communism, our life today, the starving, Bosnia – what madness! And
why, why? This sorrow, it burns inside me. I cannot shake it off.*

From Górecki's own personal angle, it was his health that suffered
most damagingly in those days. A fall when he was a small child
dislodged a hip, which ought to have been a relatively simple problem.
But his mother had died when he was only two, and in the absence of
careful supervision he received inadequate medical treatment. The hip
was improperly mended, and a sequence of operations left him with a
permanent limp. Next came tuberculosis, and again, medicines being
hard to come by during the German occupation, treatment was long-
drawn-out, arduous, and often wrong. Then, in the mid-1950s, an
infection in Górecki's fingers led one doctor to advocate amputation,
but the young composer-pianist escaped with two more operations
instead, though a tumour in his skull was yet another result of all the
medicaments he had been forced to take.

'That I'm alive is a miracle', Górecki has remarked. Equally
miraculous is the determination that enabled him to overcome the
inevitable delays first in his general education and then in his music
studies. If nothing in his early musical progress could quite match the
drama of Penderecki's threefold competition success in 1959, he did
enjoy a signal distinction at an even earlier age. On 27 February 1958
in Katowice, under Karol Stryja's direction, members of the Silesian
State Philharmonic Orchestra and a number of other musicians
devoted an entire concert to the premières of works by this 24-year-
old who had been studying music seriously for less than six years.
Among the five works played were the 1956 *Songs of Joy and Rhythm*
for two pianos and chamber orchestra and the 1957 Concerto for five

instruments and string quartet. The first was prophetic of the mature composer's élan and drive; the second showed that he had already begun to assimilate the serial lessons of Webern and other Western masters whose music was finally, with the mid-1950s cultural thaw, becoming accessible to the younger Polish generation.

The consequences of the Katowice concert were far-reaching. First Andrzej Markowski asked Górecki to write a piece for him to conduct at the Warsaw Autumn Festival that year. Titled *Epitafium* and scored for mixed choir and a small group of instruments, the resulting work now brought Górecki's name to the attention of Polish musicians in general and to the many foreign visitors always present at the festival. The performance was well received, and its success led naturally to the programming of his Symphony No. 1 for the following year's festival. This première (omitting for the moment the technically challenging second of the symphony's four movements) was given by the National Symphony Orchestra of the Polish Radio conducted by Jan Krenz on 14 September 1959, just

Right, Górecki and Penderecki at the 1961 Warsaw Autumn Festival; *above,* Górecki's *Scontri* had its première at the previous year's festival.

Górecki takes a bow after the 1960 première of *Scontri*, which was greeted with both cheers and protests.

three days before Markowski's première of *Strophes* was to introduce Penderecki to the Warsaw public.

Górecki's reputation, it is clear, was not lagging behind that of his near-exact contemporary. His status was confirmed in 1960 when *Monologhi* for soprano and three groups of instruments won first prize in the youth competition of the Union of Polish Composers, and the uninhibitedly violent gestures of *Scontri* for large orchestra aroused cheers – mingled with protests – at its Warsaw Autumn première. The following year he used some of his prize money to finance a three-month stay in Paris, where the First Symphony was promptly awarded the first prize at the second Youth Biennale, and he also visited Cologne to attend a performance of *Epitafium* conducted by Bruno Maderna, making the acquaintance of Boulez and Stockhausen while he was there.

Górecki works continued to be heard first at the Warsaw Autumn. Severino Gazzelloni introduced the *Three Diagrams* for solo flute in September 1961, and members of the Silesian State Philharmonic conducted by Karol Stryja played the second of the three pieces in the *Genesis* series, *Canti Strumentali* for fifteen players, a year later. With these works and their predecessors, Górecki was by now firmly ensconced in the minds of the Warsaw Autumn public as a leader of the Polish modern school, alongside Penderecki, whose *Threnody*, after winning a UNESCO prize in Paris, had its Warsaw première at the 1961 festival under Markowski's direction.

It is true that the *Genesis* piece had combined modernism with some simplification of texture and organization, focusing with a new radical intensity – as its name suggests – on the basic sound-elements that musical creation starts out from. But it was with Górecki's next Warsaw première (in April 1964, not at the Autumn Festival) that his style was seen to be fundamentally changing. Composed in 1963, the Three Pieces in Old Style for string orchestra were written (according to Adrian Thomas, who has made an exhaustive study of Górecki's output) 'in response to a gentle jibe that he couldn't write tuneful music'.

A composer – it hardly needs saying – doesn't change his musical character as the result of such a banal incident. When Erik Satie, sixty years earlier, 'refuted' Debussy's accusation of formlessness by titling a composition *Trois Morceaux en forme de poire*, he was being utterly true to his eccentric but deep-seated sense of humour. And Górecki's

response to his mocking associate was in its turn the expression of
a need already implicit in his music, though perhaps not yet
perceived. In any case, the newly central role allotted in the last of the
Three Pieces to a sixteenth-century Polish wedding song, and the
radical simplicity of language and treatment throughout the work,
proved to be no momentary aberration but a move that would define
Górecki's creative purpose for at least the next three decades.

It is curious, or maybe just indicative of the ambiguity of all such
stylistic matters, that the move should have come in the same year as
Górecki's one brief visit to the Summer Courses at Darmstadt (where
Michael Gielen conducted the first complete performance of the First
Symphony) and at a time when he was thinking about studying with
Luigi Nono, an uncompromising modernist. He decided instead to
spend another three months in Paris. Here he renewed his
acquaintance with Boulez, and went again every Sunday to hear
Messiaen play the organ at St Trinité. Despite what has occasionally
been stated in print, Górecki did not in the event study with
Messiaen, and he has told me that it was not until 1980 that he had
any real opportunity to talk to him. But he has consistently named
Messiaen, sometimes in tandem with Charles Ives, as the greatest
twentieth-century master. 'After Messiaen', he declared in a rare 1993
television interview, 'it's all finished for me'. The pairing of Messiaen
with Ives may at first sight seem an odd one. But Ives's Protestant
Yankee transcendentalism, while far removed in sectarian terms from
Messiaen's Roman Catholic ritual fervour, shares with it a frank
acceptance of mystical extremism, and the two men also have in
common an exuberant delight in the exploitation of music's
fundamental sonorities for their own sensual effect, quite distinct
from any element of intellectual elaboration.

Górecki's next work, *Choros I*, also scored for string orchestra,
was first performed in Warsaw in September 1964, and *Refrain* for
orchestra became the first substantial Górecki piece to have its
première outside Poland when Pierre Colombo conducted it in
Geneva in October 1965. Thus by the middle of the decade the two
leading Polish composers of their generation were both fully
established at home and becoming so abroad.

That Górecki did not at this point go on to acquire the kind of
international celebrity that was Penderecki's after the *St Luke Passion*

The composer and
conductor Pierre Boulez,
already a dominant figure
in Paris in the 1960s

Above, the Italian composer and Schoenberg's son-in-law, Luigi Nono, and *right,* Olivier Messiaen; Górecki, who at one time thought of studying with Nono, regarded Messiaen as the last of the great masters.

was the result less of musical quality than of character and of differing attitudes to what is called 'career development'. In fostering the latter, showing yourself to audiences – meeting people, establishing a personal presence – may not be as important a factor as talent, but it helps. Penderecki almost always went where his music was being performed: Górecki almost never did. Górecki moreover – and this again was a result of character difference – did not produce a work for the dedication of the Auschwitz monument in April 1967, and Penderecki did.

In fact, as David Drew has recounted, it was Górecki who suggested that Penderecki should be asked to take over this commitment when he himself found he could not fulfil it at the time. It was not that the subject did not interest him: it was that it interested him too consumingly to be worthily handled, at least yet. Discussing his thoughts about the project a year or so later, Górecki told the musicologist Tadeusz Marek:

This work has been germinating in my mind for years, troubling me, yet clamouring for its realization. I want to write it, I want to be capable of writing it – and that unfortunately is all I can say about it just now.

For the moment, then, what came out of the invitation from the director of the Auschwitz Museum was not a Górecki work, but Penderecki's *Dies Irae*. Górecki put his plans, which at that time involved five soprano soloists and a massive choral and orchestral apparatus, on one side. They were not to be realized for another nine years, and then in somewhat different shape. In the meantime he worked on a variety of other pieces, and the new focus of interest set by the Three Pieces in Old Style was at once sharpened and diversified.

The series of ensemble pieces that appeared under the title *Musiquette* between 1967 and 1970 were in diametrical opposition to the monumental concerns that had been preoccupying Górecki. Feeling a nostalgia for the kind of 'ordinary musical statements that "enlarge", so to speak, the character, features, and mood of everyday life', he described the *Musiquettes* to Marek as not a flight from 'big themes' but rather as 'an attempt to rehabilitate those 'minor problems' which at a certain moment or in a specific situation may turn out to be, for the composer, the most important problems.'

In this regard the *Musiquettes* take their logical place as an extension of the *Genesis* series' examination of musical foundation-stones. The same period produced two orchestral works. The first of these, premièred at the Warsaw Autumn Festival in 1969 under Andrzej Markowski, has become one of Górecki's best-known compositions. Titled *Old Polish Music*, it greatly extended the procedure of incorporating ancient materials in his textures and forms. Then came *Canticum Graduum*, purely orchestral despite its title, which brought him another foreign première when it was introduced by Michael Gielen in Düsseldorf in December 1969.

At the beginning of the 1970s, *Ad Matrem* for soprano, chorus, and orchestra, to the composer's own Latin text, and Two Sacred Songs, to Polish texts by Marek Skwarnicki, marked a decisive new emphasis on the human voice. Only three of Górecki's first twenty-eight works had been vocal: from *Ad Matrem* onwards, twenty-five of the thirty-nine composed between 1971 and 1994 were to use voices.

The very next of these, Symphony No. 2 for soprano and baritone soloists, chorus, and orchestra, dwarfs most of the others not only in duration (it is about thirty-five minutes long) but also in the forces it uses and the scope of the ideas it addresses. Subtitled *Copernican*, it

Among Poland's World War II ruins stood the monument to the astronomer Nicolaus Copernicus, who inspired Górecki's Second Symphony.

was commissioned by the Kosciuszko Foundation to celebrate the 500th anniversary of the birth of Nicolaus Copernicus. For his brief text, Górecki aptly juxtaposed an excerpt from the Polish astronomer's *De revolutionibus orbium coelestium* describing the all-embracing beauty of the heavens with sentences from the Psalms celebrating God's creation of heaven and earth and the great lights, sun, moon, and stars. Written on huge manuscript pages, with as many as fifty-eight staves in places to accommodate the profuse subdivisions of the string parts, the score attains a cosmic vastness of sound and gesture commensurate with its subject. The message of the work seems quintessentially Góreckian in its untroubled juxtaposition of scientific with traditionally religious concepts. At the same time, the choice of a Polish textual source for one of the composer's grandest inspirations is far from being merely coincidental: sophisticated Polish intellect and peasant Polish faith are here fused under the banner of an

Unlike the conventional 'ivory tower' idea of a composer, Górecki revels in life among country people. *Above,* Gorecki converses with neighbouring farmers; *right,* workmanship like that of a Zakopane woodcarver is a valued part of his heritage.

understandably comprehensive national pride.

The Second Symphony was first performed in Warsaw under Markowski's direction in June 1973, and had its American première in Minneapolis soon after. Górecki, who had already won a competition in Szczecin with his 1968 Cantata for organ, was now awarded the first prize of the UNESCO International Composers' Rostrum in Paris for his *Ad Matrem*, and in the same year he received the latest of three awards from the Polish Ministry of Culture. A still higher national honour, the State Award of the First Degree, went in 1976 to *Ad Matrem* and the Second Symphony jointly.

On the domestic front, meanwhile, the Góreckis had had two children, both of whom showed early signs of musical talent. Anna (who in 1993 recorded the piano version of her father's 1980 Harpsichord Concerto) was born on 19 June 1967, and Mikołaj (who as a child premièred the Three Little Pieces for violin and piano with his mother accompanying for an examination at the Katowice Academy) on 1 February 1971. Katowice remained the family's settled home, but Górecki had acquired the habit of renting a summer house in Chochołow, in the Tatra mountain region. Walking and talking with the farmers about country concerns, he felt closer here to the peasant roots that have always been vital to him, and here some of his most relaxed musical thinking has been done. As well as the farmers, Górecki observes that there are – again, in the peasant tradition – many artists in the area:

I talk to many painters – if I weren't a composer myself, I would be a pianist, and if not a pianist, then a painter. And there's a wonderful woodcarver from Zakopane whom we know well. All these things I use in my music.

The only other major sortie abroad during this period was to Berlin. Górecki spent some time there in 1973–4 on a fellowship offered (like Penderecki's five years earlier) by the German Academic Exchange Service, but during this residence a serious illness interrupted his composing plans. An interruption of another nature came in 1975, when he accepted the post of Principal at the Katowice Academy of Music. He held it for four years, but by that time political tensions were building up in Poland. When the pressures on him

*Opposite, in complete
contrast to rural idylls is the
highly industrialized
environment of Górecki's
native Silesian coal region.*

came to a head in 1979 Górecki – evidently, like Panufnik, not a man
adept at compromise – resigned in protest, and for the next few years
withdrew from all public activity.

What led to this step was, he has explained, a combination of
political and religious factors:

> *Silesia was much more oppressed by the Party than Kraków or
> Warsaw. Katowice was a new city, industrial: the coal industry – workers,
> workers, workers. According to the Party, what they ought to do was just
> work and be stupid. It was hard to found a university there. At that time
> the Music Academy was the oldest high school there – it was fifty years old.
> All intellectual movements were seen as dangerous to the Party. You can't
> imagine in the West what a pressure the Party, the Russians, the Soviets
> were … When Arvo Pärt, the Estonian composer, first came to Poland
> with a group of Soviet composers, he wasn't permitted to meet any Polish
> composers. That was strictly forbidden!*

Onto this already volatile scene there now entered the
unprecedented figure of a Polish Pope, complicating Górecki's
position still further:

> *I had been commissioned to write a piece by the Pope – well, when he
> commissioned it he was still a cardinal. It was a piece to commemorate the
> 900th anniversary of the martyrdom of St Stanisław. Then the cardinal
> suddenly became Pope. And when the Party hierarchy discovered that I
> was in the organizing committee for his visit, and that I was writing a
> piece for him, there was a great outcry.*
>
> *It was the Music Academy's jubilee year. I was the Principal, but I was
> no Principal – no music by Górecki was to be performed for the jubilee.
> And the Party people were always asking: 'Who's studying with Górecki?'
> So that's the answer to the question why I resigned.*
>
> *I conducted the première of the new piece* [Beatus Vir] *myself in the
> cathedral in Kraków, in the presence of the Pope. That was the only
> concert of my music. But the Secretary of the Party has been dead now
> these many years.*

*Following page, Górecki
acknowledges applause
after a performance of
Scontri at the Warsaw
Festival in 1960.*

Ever since the 1960s premières of the Three Pieces in Old Style
and *Old Polish Music*, and all through the 1970s with the appearance

of works like *Ad Matrem*, and the Second and Third Symphonies, Górecki's critical reputation had been growing more and more controversial. Pro and con parties were drawn up to each side of him much as they were for Penderecki. The work he had written for the Pope, the expansive *Beatus Vir* for baritone, chorus, and orchestra, simply continued in this line, only injecting a political element into the artistic battleground. But perhaps because he had not attained the same degree of international visibility as his colleague, Górecki had a harder time coping with the political pressures of the 1980s – or at least, was either less interested or less successful in making his musical voice heard. In 1981 he wrote a huge *Miserere* for unaccompanied chorus, and dedicated it to the city of Bydgoszcz, where some of the worst clashes between Solidarity activists and the security forces had taken place. For six years, the work had no chance of performance. When it was eventually premièred, in St Stanisław's Church in Włocławek in September 1987, the authorities prevented any public announcement of the event – but every seat was occupied.

The tide was turning for Górecki in a number of ways. Two months before the *Miserere* performance, his *Totus Tuus*, a shorter but scarcely less important unaccompanied choral piece composed for Pope John Paul II's third return to his homeland, had been heard both directly and by loudspeaker relay at the High Mass celebrated by the Pontiff before vast crowds in Victory Square, Warsaw. And there were promising developments outside Poland too.

Górecki portrayed on a 1989 visit to London

In 1983 and 1984, the English scholar Adrian Thomas's articles in *Contact* both signalled and helped to develop a new awareness of Górecki in Western musical circles. In July 1984, travelling abroad for the first time since the Berlin visit eleven years earlier, he accepted an invitation to the annual music festival and workshop at Lerchenborg Castle near Kalundborg in Denmark. Here the Fynske Trio gave the première (incomplete, since a recurrence of illness had delayed the composition) of *Recitatives and Ariosos – Lerchenmusik* for clarinet, cello, and piano, commissioned in connection with his visit as principal guest of that year's composing workshop. The complete première followed two months later at the Warsaw Autumn Festival. In 1986 the international publishing house Boosey & Hawkes began an association with Górecki that was to help in the wider dissemination of his music. A more ambitious agreement, giving the firm rights in all future works, followed in 1993, and in February 1994 Górecki signed a remarkable agreement with the Elektra Nonesuch record company setting up plans for a Composer's Edition to be recorded under his supervision.

Górecki wrote his first string quartet, *Already it is Dusk*, in 1988 for the Kronos Quartet, which premièred it in Minneapolis the following January, played it all over the world, recorded it for the Nonesuch label, and commissioned a second work in the genre, *Quasi una Fantasia*, first performed in Cleveland, Ohio, in October 1991 and also quickly recorded. The association with the Kronos Quartet fuelled suspicions in some quarters about the purity of Górecki's artistic intentions, for the Kronos has the reputation of a trendy if brilliant group. In September 1989, furthermore, with a performance at St Magnus Church in Braunschweig to commemorate the fiftieth anniversary of the outbreak of World War II, the hitherto dormant Third Symphony suddenly awoke and burst on the world, with the consequences already described.

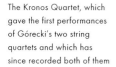

The Kronos Quartet, which gave the first performances of Górecki's two string quartets and which has since recorded both of them

In what by now remains of the serious 'new music' camp the symphony itself, like the Kronos trappings of the two quartets, came in for some opprobrium for supposedly 'New Age' tendencies. But what all Górecki's latest works, from *Good Night* composed in memory of Michael Vyner in 1990 and the Second String Quartet, *Quasi una Fantasia*, of 1990–91 down to the Concerto-Cantata for flute and orchestra written in 1992 for Carol Wincenc and the *Kleines Requiem für eine Polka* written for Reinbert de Leeuw and the Schönberg Ensemble in 1993, may have in common with 'New Age' music is no more than a willingness to take its time and an unmistakably hypnotic quality.

How such characteristics fit into the pattern of Górecki's development over the past forty years we shall consider in Chapter 6. What is worth stressing here is the clarity of all his statements about the relations between composer and public, or about music in general and his place in it, and their consistency with the way he has lived as a composer since emerging from his formative period around 1960. As he put it in the Dutch television documentary made in connection with the première of the *Kleines Requiem* in 1993:

This caricature of Górecki by Trog of *The Observer* appeared in 1993, in the wake of the Third Symphony's unprecedented public success.

> *You don't write for the drawer. You have to find someone who's willing to play it, and of course people who'll listen. It's a pretty sad business, if you just compose from festival to festival – from Donaueschingen to Darmstadt, from Darmstadt to Warsaw, from Warsaw to Freiburg … The directors of the festivals always need new works, but what does it amount to? Pieces to perform once and then throw away.*
>
> *I listen to the radio a lot. But not contemporary music. I still find so many new things in Mozart, and Schubert – new things that interest me, that I need, that give me answers to questions. I don't find that in contemporary music. Maybe I'm too stupid or something … Of course I know a lot of my colleagues' work, but I always come back to Schubert, to Mozart, and to Messiaen and Ives. Messiaen you can't listen to every day. But Mozart and Bach – I play some of that every day. That's bread, good wholewheat bread; daily bread, that's what Mozart and Bach are.*
>
> *The Third Symphony? Well, yes, I'm glad that happened for me, but it's in the past. 'Enormous success', yes, all right. But then I think of Mozart and Schubert … So I say, 'Dear friend, there are no pockets in*

With soprano soloist Dawn
Upshaw, Górecki listens
to a playback at the May
1991 recording of his Third
Symphony in London.

*your last shirt – you don't take anything with you under the ground'. So
thanks, but I must get on with it, and see that I get my little notes on
paper. If you've talked with death as often as I have, then you say, 'Third
Symphony, okay – bye-bye!' There are more important things in life.*

Henryk Górecki wanted, as we have seen, to write a work about
Auschwitz. But he also asked, back in 1968, whether the *problem* of
Auschwitz might not embrace more than the *subject* of Auschwitz, and
he has himself cautioned against too narrow an interpretation of the
Third Symphony, despite the sources and references of its texts:

*Many of my family died in concentration camps. I had a grandfather
who was in Dachau, an aunt in Auschwitz. You know how it is between
Poles and Germans. But Bach was a German too – and Schubert, and
Strauss. Everyone has his place on this little earth. That's all behind me.
So the Third Symphony is not about war, it's not a Dies Irae; it's a normal*
Klagenliedersinfonie ['Symphony of Sorrowful Songs'].

It is important, in considering the use Górecki has made of
wartime associations, to distinguish his own response from that of
some of those who have taken it upon themselves to publicize his
work. Tony Palmer's film, for example, intercut the most horrifying
footage of concentration camps and of African famine victims with

In his Katowice study,
Górecki is surrounded by
the icons of Christianity and
the craftsmen's work that
he loves.

shots of the soprano Dawn Upshaw singing the Third Symphony; the result, at least in the eyes of this viewer, overstepped the legitimate bounds of art or even decent journalism, injecting into a universal tragedy an element that seemed merely facile.

The composer himself has never lost sight of the universal aspect. 'Those things are too immense – you can't write music about them', he has said of the events of the Second World War. Yet in a way his reach and grasp in this quintessential work are more immense still. Philosophically, the Third Symphony confronts the theme of suffering in its most unchanging aspect.

Górecki misses few opportunities to talk about his veneration of Schubert. Rather like Handel (who, Beethoven remarked, knew how to produce 'the greatest effects with the simplest means'), Schubert stands as one of Górecki's spiritual ancestors in his gift for turning simplicity to profoundly human ends. It is ironic that, in a work like the Third Symphony, Polish music found a universal language by rejecting the facile orthodoxies of modish modernism on the one hand and dogmatically programmed 'social realism' on the other. Ironic, but not surprising, for the way to the heart has always been through individual thought and feeling, not through the collectivist cant of either artistic schools or political structures.

6

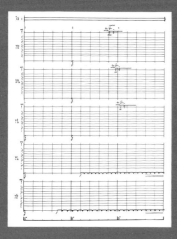

Penderecki's 1962 Canon
for strings and recorded
tape exemplifies his use of
notation in specific units
of time rather than in
conventional rhythmic units.

*Krzysztof Penderecki, Wojciech Kilar, and
Henryk Mikołaj Górecki made the most
spectacular composing debuts in Poland at the
end of the 1950s. Although the poetic content of
each one's work differed from the start, the
direction of their development had much in
common. This was evident in the seventies,
when their music stood on the brink of the next
upheaval ... One characteristic that all three
had in common should be noted: Krzysztof
Penderecki was already writing religious music
in the mid sixties, Wojciech Kilar and Henryk
Mikołaj Górecki from the beginning of the
seventies. Their return to these sources coincided
with their turning away from the sonic
radicalism of their earlier compositions.*

Andrzej Chłopecki, 'Faces of
Postmodernism', *Musiktexte* No. 44,
April 1992

Penderecki and Górecki: Commentary

Witold Lutosławski was once asked, after a concert of his music in Philadelphia, how as a conductor he approached the task of preparing and performing one of his own works. His reply was: 'I conduct the work of my younger colleague, whom I know probably better than any other conductor'. In the light of that answer, it is interesting to consider what sort of composers early Penderecki or early Górecki must look like to Penderecki and Górecki now.

Both men at the start of their careers wrote music essentially different from anything either has produced in the last thirty years, and to a cursory eye the respective transformations of style may seem to have followed a broadly similar course. Below the surface, however, is a fundamental difference between their temperaments and artistic identities. Once again, as with Lutosławski and Panufnik, we are confronted on the one hand with synthesis and diversification, and on the other with reduction, concentration, and the urge for unity.

Any young Polish composition student at the end of the 1960s was faced with the necessity of absorbing several decades of music history all at once. A highly intellectual modernist movement was spreading around the world at that time from influential centres like Darmstadt. Much of it revolved around the idea of 'total serialism'. This was an attempt at widely extending the organizing methods that Schoenberg and his disciples had applied to pitch. The idea was to take all the other aspects of music (such as rhythm, dynamics, articulation, and tone-colour) out of the province of the composer's moment-to-moment 'inspiration' and subject them instead to systematic control.

Like many others in Poland and elsewhere, Penderecki and Górecki were naturally swept along at the outset on this aesthetic current. But their music, if you listen to it carefully, shows that they did not both react in quite the same way. Górecki was the truer believer – at first. His commitment to serialist principles went further; his application of the movement's organizing techniques was more thorough and affected a greater number of works. Serial methods can

Opposite, the fragmented textures of Górecki's First Symphony proved so taxing for performers that one movement was omitted at the work's 1959 Warsaw Autumn première.

be traced in compositions from his student days, and they still play
their part in the way the materials 'quoted' from fourteenth- and
sixteenth-century sources are treated texturally as late as his Opus 24,
the *Old Polish Music* completed in 1969. Here old and new are
blended in a complex mix of textures and sonorities that refracts
barbaric grandeur through the prism of an unmistakably
modern sensibility.

By the same token, Górecki's reaction against the modernist
orthodoxy was, when it came, more extreme than Penderecki's. One of
the central tenets of serialism from its earliest days had been the
avoidance of note-repetition. Nothing could be more characteristic of
the mature Górecki style than the insistent – indeed, positively
obsessional – repetition of notes. The taste for simplicity, dominating
his music increasingly from about 1963 onwards, led to a new
willingness to let folk materials speak for themselves. It was a taste
utterly opposed to the drive towards complication evident in the
serialists – except perhaps Webern – from the start, and more
obtrusive than ever in 1950s and 60s serialism.

Notice I do not say 'complexity': one of the problems in discussing
simplicity is that there are two words, both seemingly its opposites,
but quite distinct from each other in meaning: 'complexity' and
'complication'. There is no lack of complexity in Webern, but his
music is hardly ever complicated. There is a good deal of complication
in serialist or modernist works from Schoenberg by way of Boulez to
Ferneyhough, but too often also a stultifying lack of complexity.
Perhaps the true opposition is between 'simple' and 'complicated', not
between 'simple' and 'complex'. Few composers, after all, are either
simpler than Schubert (to take just one example) or more complex.

For Penderecki, as is clear when we look back at his music around
1960, serial techniques were a useful expedient, not a creative
foundation. They generally played a rather small constructional role,
in a rather small number of works, and when Penderecki moved away
from them, his movement was correspondingly less than extreme. The
reason in both cases is basic to an understanding of his music.

Penderecki fundamentally a dramatist, and his concern is with
effect – not 'mere effects', but the effect of music on the listener
insofar as the composer can envisage and plan for it. He is instinctual
in method, and seizes the discoveries of others, as composers have

been doing for centuries, whenever they suit his purpose ('I take what I can use'). His legitimate annexations from the common stock of musical language have ranged over the centuries. He uses Stravinskyan rhythm, Bachian counterpoint, Second-Viennese-School twelve-note series, noise-constructs *à la* Varèse, and Xenakis's glissandos and clouds of sonority, just as he uses the legacies of folk song and Gregorian chant. Their interest for him derives purely and specifically from their appropriateness to his expressive needs.

As those needs have changed, so Penderecki's stylistic outlook has shifted. Between about the time of the *Stabat Mater* in 1962 and that of the Violin Concerto and *Paradise Lost* towards the end of the 1970s, the trend of his evolution was away from serialism and noise and correspondingly towards a rapprochement with the traditions of both the distant and the more recent Romantic past. Subsequently the nineteenth century has continued to exercise its sway (under a strikingly Brucknerian guise in the fitfully vehement but pervasively dark-hued Second Symphony and the Passacaglia and Adagio of Symphonies Nos. 3 and 4). But at the same time such works as the opera *The Black Mask* have explored an early-twentieth-century vein of expressionism well matched to Penderecki's often lugubrious choice of subjects, and he has also sought to reintroduce into a now predominantly neo-romantic idiom some of the harsher and more outlandish sonorities that marked his early works. Since 1990 there has been a perceptible lightening of touch. *Ubu Rex* is by some margin the least portentous of the four operas; the Fifth Symphony, while still substantial in scale, allows more relaxation than its predecessors. A new emphasis on chamber-music forms has produced, in the String Trio and the Clarinet Quartet, echoes of the elliptical manner of a work like Hans Werner Henze's Fifth String Quartet, though certainly not of its content: whereas Henze's memorable simplicities emulate the gnomic utterances of the late Beethoven quartets, Penderecki has himself, in the case of the Clarinet Quartet, claimed kinship rather with the more purely lyrical style of Schubert.

Perhaps this latest trend is a sign that we shall find Penderecki looking inwards more as he moves through his sixties. But for most of his composing life the gaze has, rather, been outwards. The fashioning of his language and style has been a process of accumulation, of accretion, even though his musical personality has been strong and distinct enough to allow him to put an individual stamp on what he has taken and used.

If Penderecki, characteristically, has added on, Górecki has taken away. His creative trajectory since that same period of omnivorous absorption before 1963 is a sustained feat of peeling away the extraneous, and revealing in its clearest, purest form what was there all along. The notion of building a style by 'taking what you can use' would surely strike him as an absurdity. For where Penderecki looks outside, Górecki compulsively looks, not merely within, but as it were underneath himself.

In a stimulating article, 'Faces of Postmodernism', published in the journal *Musiktexte* in 1992, Andrzej Chłopecki singled out Górecki from among his colleagues for his capacity of bringing together various distinct groups of listeners (elitists, 'philharmonics', and the mass audience). He tellingly added, 'probably because, in his musical search for the religious element, he comes closest to the archetypes'.

It is in the light of archetypes that Górecki's own characteristic use of the device of quotation can best be seen. When he alludes to a Chopin mazurka in the Third Symphony, or to Beethoven's Fourth Piano Concerto in *Recitatives and Ariosos,* or to Franz Xaver Gruber's famous Christmas song *Stille Nacht* in the Second String Quartet, *Quasi una Fantasia,* he does so with the utmost casualness. Penderecki uses the same Gruber tune in his Second Symphony, and the difference in the two men's methods is instructive. Where Penderecki emphatically isolates the quotation, and works on it, Górecki on such occasions is at pains not to emphasize the quoted material in any way: 'These and all such classic tags', he seems to be saying, 'are simply part of us – of you the listener and me the composer. They are there all the time in the collective unconscious, so why should we make a fuss about remembering them?'

Opposite, the last of the Third Symphony's three slow movements illustrates how far Górecki had travelled by 1976 from the disjunct rhythms of his earlier music.

There is indeed something Jungian about Górecki's progressively simplified language, his rhythmic élan, his taste for extremes of loud and soft, his luminous concentration, his quest for artistic bedrock. Penderecki, with his predilection for dark, heavily laden sonorities, his penchant for rigorous motivic processes and near-neurotic dramatic subjects, his fascinated compulsion to return again and again to the examination of physical and mental pain – Penderecki is surely much closer to the world of Freud.

Ej ćwier-kej-cie mu tam, wy pto-sec-ki bo — ze, kie — dy ma-mu-lic—ka

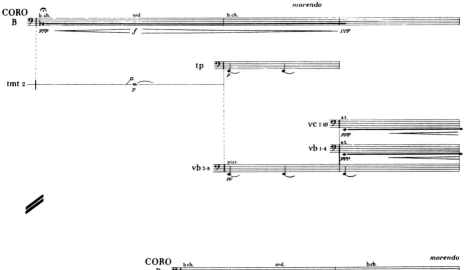

The *Dies Irae*, written to commemorate the victims of Auschwitz, is one of those works in which Penderecki, from the late 1960s on, leavened his former iconoclasm with more traditional elements.

These two careers, Penderecki's reaching a peak of public acclaim remarkably early and Górecki's a quarter of a century later, have thus also followed artistic courses more different than might be thought. The production of both men has been prolific, Penderecki's the more so. They have at the same time enjoyed the benefits and suffered the criticisms that come when familiar lines of demarcation between artistic genres, and between clearly defined publics, are overstepped.

'New Age' tendencies and minimalist elements have both been imputed to Górecki. Yet his powerful sense of concentration has nothing to do with the mental languor, the relentless relaxation, of 'New Age' music. So far as minimalism is concerned, as Adrian Thomas has put it,

*with the exception of the tongue-in-cheek Harpsichord Concerto, he
has eschewed the seductions of the repetitive rhythmic processes, single
Affekt, and beguiling timbres of his American contemporaries. For all its
apparent simplicity, his music is deeply involved with the psyche of
twentieth-century man.*

And together with his ability to compress and concentrate the
listener's experience of time to a point where all motion is suspended,
the richness of musical character that Górecki draws from his sources
of inspiration in folk art, village life, and pantheistic faith has
prompted Andrzej Chłopecki to speak rather of 'a certain maximalism'
in his work.

That static quality is what sets Górecki sharply apart from
Panufnik, whose structures are always going on to the next phase in a
way that Górecki's suspension of temporal progression avoids – where
Panufnik's music evolves, Górecki's more often revolves. It is also the
only thing, beyond mere circumstantial trifles, that he occasionally has
in common with Penderecki.

Górecki and Penderecki both completed works called *Epitafium* in
1958 (the same year, incidentally, in which Lutosławski finished his
Funeral Music); they both wrote works called Three Pieces in Old
Style in 1963; they both wrote flute concertos in 1992. But the
coincidences, if striking, are insignificant, because there is no real
affinity between the works in each pair. 'Old', for instance, in the
sense Penderecki applies in his Three Pieces, refers to a purposely
artificial Baroque antiquity much more recent than the magically
distant Renaissance of Górecki's inspiration. The far-reaching effects
of the Industrial Revolution on man's psyche are always somehow
implicit in Penderecki's music – he is what might in this context be
called a sophisticated, a *knowing*, artist – whereas Górecki's
imagination achieves a clear backward leap to an earlier, more
innocent phase in the human condition.

What is more interesting is the *artistic* characteristic they share,
though they have it from widely different sources. Górecki's creation
of new kinds of musical material (blocks and sheets of sonority,
smudged lines, dynamic masses, that all subordinate the individual
note in a more comprehensive sonic unit) conduces to a quasi-

Penderecki had moved a long way back in the direction of Romantic rhetoric by the time he wrote his Viola Concerto in 1983.

mystical sense of immobility, and his frequent juxtaposition of frenetically violent assertion with near-inaudible reticence intensifies this effect. Penderecki's pervasive chromaticism also, though not deployed with the systematic approach of Lutosławski, for the most part similarly precludes any kind of rapid harmonic pulse, and so most of his music likewise tends towards immobility.

Around 1960 Penderecki devised a new way of notating the time element. From then on, in place of the 'periodic' rhythmic pulsation indicated by traditional bar-lines, many of his scores offer the performer spans of specific numbers of seconds, which have no metrical significance. In orchestral performance, the consequence is that rather than 'beating time' the conductor is required to control it simply by giving specific cues to the players. (In Chicago in 1969 I witnessed a performance of the *Threnody* in which the conductor, presumably having renotated the score for the sake of what he thought of as the players' ease and convenience, insisted on giving what looked like regular beats throughout. The inevitable result, since listeners are not blind and it is natural to assimilate what one hears to what one sees, was that the audience heard the piece in a completely misleading way.)

Specifying seconds may seem to imply a greater rather than a smaller interest in temporal progression, but paradoxically it has the opposite effect. Saying 'now do this for seven seconds – now do that for eleven seconds' is actually a more cavalier way of treating time than building it into a periodic metrical pattern, and it is not surprising that Penderecki often combines the new technique with stretches of the old, and in many works abandons it altogether.

In his most cataclysmic vein, Penderecki can conjure up through his music all the elemental power of a battle of gods and giants, but it is a battle frozen somewhere outside time – we can never know the result. This, rather than any supposed pandering to popular taste, is why in some of his 1960s pieces the recourse to a juicy common chord by way of conclusion seemed to go beyond even the most generously drawn boundaries of legitimate eclecticism: those big major-key affirmations came as words from a foreign language in which time's progress is depicted in perfectly normal terms.

Conversely, a work like the *Threnody*, playing by the rules all the way to the end, can still after more than thirty years compel our admiration. For in such works Penderecki deploys his strange, vehement, hostile, frightening, yet wistful and touching sound-constructions in a way at once consistent and utterly convincing. In the process he creates a new kind of movement, which is not musical movement in the traditional sense, but can effectively replace it through sheer dramatic intensity.

Such effects speak most strongly and with the most unmistakable individuality in the first phases of Penderecki's outward journey towards new creative stimuli. For so resourceful a composer, and one only just past sixty, it would be rash to predict the shape of the future. But among the production of his first four composing decades, it is in works like the *Threnody* and *Polymorphia*, and still also in the *St Luke Passion*, that the listener will find his most characteristic voice. Notice that the latest of the pieces just named was written as long ago as 1966. There are incidental felicities to be found in many of Penderecki's more recent works. Yet it is hard – at the risk of a premature judgement – not to conclude that in his case the turn away from early modernist extremes betokened in part the desperate seeking of a man who has mined his vein of creativity too comprehensively too soon.

With Górecki's journey towards his own centre, on the other hand, while such pieces as the First Symphony and *Scontri* stand as notable idiosyncratic achievements, they only hint at the unique personality that was in the wings. The Second and Third Symphonies and *Beatus Vir* focused that uniqueness sharply.

Then Górecki, with his habitual unconcern for career, turned away from the attractions of the big public and the big concert hall. He has written only one piece that uses full orchestral forces since 1979, but in his later chamber music, including *Recitatives and Ariosos*, *Good Night*, and the two string quartets, and on the medium scale of the *Kleines Requiem für eine Polka*, he has given us his essence. Whereas Penderecki's ceaseless search for new creative stimuli seems to have diminished his own artistic size, Górecki, by burrowing ever more deeply within himself, has grown to world stature.

Postlude

Drawing up balance-sheets of artistic achievement is an occupation of questionable utility to the present-day observer, and its validity for the future is even more dubious. A prediction, around 1950, that Lutosławski would soon be Poland's leading composer might well have been thought absurd: as most people knew, that distinction belonged to Panufnik. Then in 1954 Panufnik left for his long exile in England, and became a non-person at home, and Lutosławski succeeded to his position at the top. From then on, intelligent Polish musicians might similarly have discounted a prediction that Panufnik's music would again one day be regularly performed and cheered at the Warsaw Autumn Festival (assuming they even knew who Panufnik was). Yet eventually, starting with the performance of *Universal Prayer* in 1977, that happened too.

Similar shifts of fortune have occurred with all four composers. Lutosławski himself went through discouragements enough in the difficult circumstances of the first ten years under Communism (not to speak of the impossible circumstances of the Nazi period). Penderecki's popularity with audiences has admittedly been more or less uninterrupted since his first spectacular success in 1959, but his critical reputation has covered the gamut from adulation to positively virulent denigration. Górecki could easily have spent the years between 1960 and 1992 wondering whether he would ever reach the wide public his communicative urge demanded (except that he does not seem the kind of man to worry about such things); and then, through a recording of the Third Symphony, the least widely known of our four composers suddenly outstripped the others in celebrity.

It is sad how easily history can be forgotten or rewritten. In the notes for a 1993 recording of music by Górecki, a German commentator tells us that 'from 1958 the annual Warsaw Autumn Festival became a veritable Mecca of the avant garde, a place to which composers and musicians from throughout the world made pilgrimages' – and the composers he lists among those they came to hear include Panufnik, in fact unplayed there for nearly twenty years. But it is true that, below the surface represented by public performance or in Panufnik's case the lack of it, scholars and students were beginning to take an interest in the banned composer by the beginning of the 1970s. A 1984 article in *Tempo* by the British composer, writer, and student of Polish music Nigel Osborne describes his experience as a member of a composition class at the Warsaw Conservatoire in 1970. After the usual analysis of recent works by Penderecki, Lutosławski, Górecki, Serocki, and others, Osborne relates:

> *One day, when we had been discussing microtonal music, our instructor produced two yellowing and dog-eared scores from his briefcase and laid them reverently before us on the table. 'Now, ladies and gentlemen, if you really want to see the first example of this technique in Polish music, look here', he said, opening the first page of* Lullaby, *'and remember, this is a work written in 1947'. There it was, rather like looking at one of Leonardo's aeroplanes, a forgotten prototype of Polish School texture, created some twenty years ahead of its time: silvery wisps of tremolo quarter tones, unfolding across each other, settling like mist around a simple diatonic line – or, as the composer has described it, like clouds passing the moon. 'And that's not all. Many if not most of the innovations of Polish contemporary music made their first appearance in the work of Andrzej Panufnik – he really was the first experimentalist'.*

The story is worth repeating because it shows how uncertain the public view of music and its creators can be at any given time. It is for this reason that any more predictions about the future reputation or influence of Panufnik, or Lutosławski, or Penderecki, or Górecki will *not* be ventured here. We don't even know (though we have our hopes, and our fears) what kind of country Poland will be in another ten years' time, or what kind of culture any of us will be living in for that matter.

What can be confidently asserted is the difference these four men have made already. For listeners, each in his own way has created new varieties of musical satisfaction and spiritual refreshment. Against the crowded backdrop of twentieth-century music history, they have turned Polish music into something it had not been since the days of

Chopin nearly two centuries ago: an art from which the composers of the world take as much in example and inspiration as they contribute to it.

That is surely enough for the present. The future will look after itself. But one last comment of Lutosławski's about Polish composers deserves attention:

They write music to be listened to and not commented on.

Better late than never, you may feel, seeing it quoted here. The next step, however, is obvious.

Classified List of Works

Dates given in parentheses in the following lists are those of composition; 'fp' indicates first public performance, details of which appear in all cases where they can be ascertained; 'fp?' indicates that this information is not obtainable from the composer, the relevant publisher, or any other source consulted. Owing partly to the political vicissitudes through which the composers lived, this happens more often here than is usually the case with twentieth-century composers. It is also due partly to the fact that many of the pieces in question are songs or small-scale chamber or instrumental pieces of the kind that can easily be performed without elaborate record-keeping or even notification.

Henryk Górecki

Orchestral

Songs of Joy and Rhythm, Op. 7, for two pianos and chamber orchestra (1956, reorchestrated 1959, revised 1990). fp Katowice, 27 February 1958; London, 8 July 1990 (revised version)

Symphony No. 1 (*1959*), Op. 14, for strings, harpsichord and percussion. fp Warsaw, 14 September 1959 (1st, 3rd and 4th movements only); Darmstadt, 1963 (complete work)

Scontri ('Collisions'), Op. 17, (1960). fp Warsaw, 21 September 1960

Three Pieces in Old Style, for strings (1963). fp Warsaw, 30 April 1964

Choros I, Op. 20, for strings (1964). fp Warsaw, 22 September 1964

Refrain, Op. 21 (1965). fp Geneva, 27 October 1965

Old Polish Music, Op. 24, for brass and strings (1967–9). fp Warsaw, 24 September 1969

Canticum Graduum, Op. 27 (1969). fp Düsseldorf, 1 December 1969

Three Dances, Op. 34 (1973). fp Rybnik, 24 November 1973

Harpsichord Concerto, Op. 40, for harpsichord (or piano) and strings (1980). fp Katowice, 2 March 1980

Concerto-Cantata, Op. 65, for flute and orchestra (1992). fp Amsterdam, 28 November 1992

Large Ensemble

Concerto, Op. 11, for five instruments and string quartet (1957). fp Katowice, 27 February 1958

Genesis 2: Canti Strumentali, Op. 19 No. 2, for fifteen players (1962). fp Warsaw, 16 September 1962

Musiquette 2, Op. 23, for four trumpets, four trombones, two pianos and percussion (1967). fp Warsaw, 23 September 1967

Kleines Requiem für eine Polka, Op. 66, for piano and thirteen instruments (1993). fp Amsterdam, 12 June 1993

Vocal

Three Songs, Op. 3, for medium voice and piano, text (in Polish) by Juliusz Słowacki and Julian Tuwim (1956). fp Cologne, 1960

Epitafium, Op. 12, for chorus and instruments, text (in Polish) by Julian Tuwim (1958). fp Warsaw, 3 October 1958

Monologhi, Op. 16, for soprano and three groups of instruments, text (in Polish) by Henryk Górecki (1960). fp Berlin, 26 April 1968

Genesis 3 Monodramma, Op. 19 No. 3, for soprano, metal percussion and six contrabasses, text (largely syllabic and wordless) by Henryk Górecki (1963). fp?

Ad Matrem, Op. 29, for soprano, chorus and orchestra, text (in Latin) by Henryk Górecki (1971). fp Warsaw, 24 September 1972

Two Sacred Songs, Op. 30, for baritone and orchestra, text (in Polish) by Marek Skwarnicki (also version for baritone and piano, Op. 30 bis) (1971). fp Poznań, 6 April 1976

Euntes Ibant et Flebant, Op. 32, for chorus, text (in Latin) from Psalms 125 and 94 (1972). fp Wrocław, 31 August 1975

Symphony No. 2 (*Copernican*)*,* Op. 31, for soprano, baritone, chorus and large orchestra, text (in Latin) from Psalms 145 and 135, and excerpt from *De revolutionibus orbium coelestium* by Nicolaus Copernicus (1972). fp Warsaw, 22 June 1973

Two Little Songs of Tuwim, Op. 33, for chorus of four equal voices, text (in Polish) by Julian Tuwim (1972). fp?

Amen, Op 35, for chorus, text (in Latin) traditional (1975). fp?

Symphony No. 3 (*Symphony of Sorrowful Songs*)*,* Op. 36, for soprano and large orchestra, old Polish religious and folk texts (1976). fp Royan, 4 April 1977

Beatus Vir, Op. 38, for baritone, chorus and large orchestra, text (in Latin) from Psalms 142, 30, 37, 66, and 33 (1979). fp Kraków, 9 June 1979

Broad Waters, Op. 39, for chorus, text (in Polish) traditional (1979). fp?

Two Songs of Lorca, Op. 42, for voice and piano, text (in Polish) by Mikołaj Bieszczadowski after Federico García Lorca (1956–80). fp?

Blessed Raspberry Songs, Op. 43, for voice and piano, text (in Polish) by Cyprian Norwid (1980). fp?

Dark Evening is Falling, Op. 45, folksongs for chorus, text (in Polish) traditional (1981). fp?

Miserere, Op. 44, for chorus, text (in Latin) liturgical (1981). fp Włocławek, 10 September 1987

My Vistula, Grey Vistula, Op. 46, folksong for chorus, text (in Polish) traditional (1981). fp Poznań, 28 April 1987

Cloud Comes, Rain Falls, Op. 51, folksong for chorus, text (in Polish) traditional, ed. Oskar Kolberg (1984). fp?

O My Little Garland of Lavender, Op. 50, folksong for chorus, text (in Polish) traditional, ed. Oskar Kolberg (1984). fp?

Three Lullabies, Op. 49, for chorus, text (in Polish) traditional (1984, revised 1991). fp Lerchenborg, Denmark, 2 August 1991

Angelus Domini, Op. 57, for chorus, text (in Polish) by Kazimierz Przerwa Tetmajer (1985). fp?

Five Marian Songs, Op. 54, for chorus, text (in Polish) traditional (1985). fp?

O Domina Nostra, Op. 55, for soprano and organ, text (in Latin) by Górecki (1985, revised 1990). fp Poznań, 31 March 1985; London, 7 July 1990 (revised version)

Under Your Protection, Op. 56, Marian Song for chorus, text (in Polish) traditional (1985). fp?

Totus Tuus, Op. 60, for chorus, text (in Latin) by Maria Bogusławska (1987). fp Warsaw, 19 July 1987

Come Holy Spirit, Op. 61, Church song for chorus, text (in Polish) traditional (1988). fp?

Good Night, Op. 63, for soprano, alto flute, piano and three tam-tams, text (in English) from Shakespeare's *Hamlet* (1990). fp London, 6 May 1990 (last movement); 4 November 1990 (complete work)

Chamber/Instrumental

Four Preludes, Op. 1, for piano (1955). fp Katowice, 30 January 1970

Toccata, Op. 2, for two pianos (1955). fp Katowice, 27 February 1958

From the Bird's Nest, Op. 9a, for piano (1956). fp?

Lullaby, Op. 9, for piano (1956). fp?

Piano Sonata No. 1 (1956, revised 1984 and 1990). fp Lerchenborg, 28 July 1984 (1st movement); Helsinki, 17 March 1991 (complete work)

Quartettino, Op. 5, for two flutes, oboe and violin (1956). fp Katowice, 27 February 1958

Variations, Op. 4, for violin and piano (1956). fp Katowice, 27 February 1958

Violin Sonatina in One Movement, Op. 8 (1956). fp after 1980

Sonata, Op. 10, for two violins (1957). fp Katowice, 27 February 1958

Five Pieces, Op. 13, for two pianos (1959). fp?

Three Diagrams, Op. 15, for flute (1959). fp Warsaw, 21 September 1961

Diagram IV, Op. 18, for flute (1961). fp?

Genesis 1: Elementi, Op. 19 No. 1, for string trio (1962). fp Kraków, 29 May 1962

Musiquette 1, Op. 22, for two trumpets and guitar (1967). fp?

Musiquette 3, Op. 25, for violas (any number of, with an minimum of three) (1967). fp Katowice, 20 October 1967

Cantata, Op. 26, for organ (1968). fp Kamień Pomorski, 18 July 1969

Musiquette 4, 'Trombone Concerto', Op 28, for trombone, clarinet, cello and piano (1970). fp Wieden, 15 April 1970

Three Little Pieces, Op. 37, for violin and piano (1977). fp Katowice, 5 January 1978

Mazurkas, Op. 41, for piano (1980). fp?

Lullabies and Dances, Op. 47, for violin and piano (1982). fp?

Recitatives and Ariosos – Lerchenmusik, Op. 53, for clarinet, cello and piano (1984–5). fp Lerchenborg, 28 July 1984 (fragment); Warsaw, 25 September 1985 (complete work)

Aria, Op. 59, for tuba, piano, tam-tam and bass drum (1987). fp?

Already it is Dusk (String Quartet No. 1), Op. 62 (1988). fp Minneapolis, Minnesota, 21 January 1989

Sundry Pieces, Op. 52, for piano: Recitative and Mazurka; Two Pieces; Three Dodecaphonic Miniatures; Quasi Valse (1956–90). fp?

For You, Anne-Lill, Op. 58, for flute and piano (1986–90). fp Lerchenborg, 4 August 1990

Intermezzo for piano (1990). fp Lerchenborg

Quasi una Fantasia (String Quartet No. 2), Op. 64 (1990–1). fp Cleveland, Ohio, 27 October 1991

Ballet

The following works are choreographed to Górecki scores (the titles are the same as the original score unless otherwise indicated).

Lament (to Symphony No. 3, 1st movement): Nacho Duato, Netherlands Dance Theatre, The Hague, 1990

Peer Gynt (to Symphony No. 3): Jochen Ulrich, Tanz-Forum, Cologne Opera, 1993

Quasi una Fantasia: Maryl Tankard, Australian Dance Theatre, 1993

Those Who Sank (to *Recitatives and Ariosos*): Tero Saarinen, Finnish National Ballet, Helsinki, 1993

Concerto (to Harpsichord Concerto): Lucinda Childs, Lucinda Childs Dance Company, USA, 1994

Crossing (to *Quasi una Fantasia*): Christopher Bruce, Rambert Dance Company, UK, 1994

Home Sweet Home (to *Quasi una Fantasia*): Jean-Christophe Maillot, Monte Carlo, 1994

Polish Pieces (to Harpsichord Concerto and Three Pieces in Old Style): Hans van Manen, Netherlands Dance Theatre, The Hague, 1994

Scheidelijn (to Symphony No. 3, 2nd movement): Ton Wiggers, Introdans, Netherlands, 1994

Spectators at an Event (to *Quasi una Fantasia*): Susan Marshall and Dancers, USA, 1994

Disregarding Changes (to Symphony No. 3, 3rd movement): Danielle Rosseels, Flanders Ballet, Belgium, 1994–5

Rif (to Symphony No. 3, 3rd movement): Mirjam Diedrich, Introdans, Netherlands, 1994–5

Eco de Silencio (to Symphony No. 3, 1st movement): Juan Carlos García, Lanomima Imperial, Brazil, 1995

She Was Black (to *Quasi una Fantasia*): Mats Ek, Cullberg Ballet, Sweden, 1995

Untitled at time of publication (to Symphony No. 3, 3rd movement): Kenneth Kvarnstrom, Finnish National Ballet, 1996

Witold Lutosławski

Much of Lutosławski's early output was lost in the Warsaw Uprising of 1944. The works in question include piano pieces from his childhood and student years, among them a Prelude (1922), *Poème* (1928), *Dance of the Chimera* (1930 – the first of his pieces to be publicly performed, in Warsaw that year), and Prelude and Aria (1936); two violin sonatas (1927); Scherzo (1930) and Double Fugue (1936) for orchestra; several sets of incidental music, including one for a 1931 production of *Haroun al Rashid* in a dramatization by Janusz Makarczyk; Two Songs, for soprano and piano, texts (in Polish) by Kazimiera Iłłakowicz, first performed in 1941 at a Warsaw café concert; and numerous film scores and children's songs. In 1937, moreover, Lutosławski wrote two sections of a Requiem as submissions for his Composition Diploma. One of these, *Requiem aeternam*, for chorus and orchestra, was likewise lost in the Uprising, the other is the *Lacrimosa* listed below.

Orchestral

Symphonic Variations (1936–8). fp Warsaw, April 1939

Symphony No. 1 (1941–7). fp Katowice, 6 April 1948

Overture for Strings (1949). fp Prague, 9 November 1949

Little Suite, for chamber orchestra (1950). fp Warsaw, 1950

Little Suite (1951 symphony orchestra revision of preceding work). fp Warsaw, 20 April 1951

Five Folk Melodies, for string orchestra (1952 arrangement of 1945 Folk Melodies for piano). fp?

Concerto for Orchestra (1950–4). fp Warsaw, 26 November 1954

Dance Preludes, for clarinet and chamber orchestra, (1955 arrangement of 1954 clarinet and piano work). fp Polish Radio, 1955; Aldeburgh, June 1963 (concert première)

Funeral Music ('Musique funèbre', 'Muzyka żałobna'), for strings (1954–8). fp Katowice, 26 March 1958

Three Postludes (1958–60, revised 1963). fp Geneva, 1 September 1963 (No. 1); Kraków, 8 October 1965 (complete work)

Jeux vénitiens ('Venetian Games'), for chamber orchestra (1960–1). fp Venice, 24 April 1961 (1st, 2nd and 4th movements); Warsaw, 16 September 1961 (complete work)

Symphony No. 2 (1965–7). fp Hamburg, 15 October 1966 (2nd movement); Katowice, 9 June 1967 (complete work)

Livre pour orchestre (1968). fp Hagen, 18 November 1968

Cello Concerto (1969–70). fp London, 14 October 1970

Preludes and Fugue, for thirteen solo strings (1970–2). fp Graz, 12 October 1972

Mi-parti (1975–6). fp Amsterdam, 22 October 1976

Variations on a Theme of Paganini, for piano and orchestra (1978 expanded orchestral version of 1941 two-piano work). fp Miami, Florida, 18 November 1979

Novelette (1978–9). fp Washington, DC, 29 January 1980

Double Concerto, for oboe, harp and chamber orchestra (two percussion and twelve string instruments) (1979–80). fp Lucerne, 24 August 1980

Grave, for cello and thirteen strings (1982 arrangement of cello and piano work). fp Paris, 26 August 1982

Symphony No. 3 (1981–3). fp Chicago, Illinois, 29 September 1983

Chain 2, dialogue for violin and orchestra (1984–5). fp Zurich, 31 January 1986

Chain 3 (1986). fp San Francisco, California, 10 December 1986

Fanfare for Louisville, for woodwind, brass, timpani and percussion (1986). fp Louisville, Kentucky, 19 September 1986

Piano Concerto (1987–8). fp Salzburg, 19 August 1988

Partita, for violin and small orchestra (1988 arrangement of 1984 violin and piano work). fp Munich, 10 January 1990 (recorded in August 1988)

Prelude for Guildhall School of Music (1989). fp London, 11 May 1989

Interlude, for small orchestra (can be played independently or as link between Partita and *Chain 2*) (1990). fp Munich, 10 January 1990

Symphony No. 4 (1988–92). fp Los Angeles, California, 5 February 1993

Vocal

Lacrimosa, for soprano, optional chorus and orchestra, text (in Latin) liturgical (1937, revised 1948). fp Warsaw, 1938

Songs of the Underground Struggle, for voice (or unison voices) and piano, text (in Polish) by Stanisław Ryszard Dobrowolski, Aleksander Maliszewski, Zofia Zawadka and anonymous (1942–4). fp?

Twenty Carols, for voice and piano, text (in Polish) traditional (1946). fp Kraków, January 1947 (Nos. 11, 15, 17, 18 and 20)

Six Children's Songs, for voice and piano, text (in Polish) by Julian Tuwim (1947). fp?

The Belated Nightingale and *About Mr Tralaliński*, for voice and piano, text (in Polish) by Julian Tuwim (1948). fp Kraków, 26 January 1948

The Snowslide, for voice and piano, text (in Polish translation) by Alexander Pushkin (1949). fp Kraków, 26 September 1950

Strawchain and Other Children's Pieces, for soprano, mezzo-soprano and five woodwind instruments, or for voice and piano, texts (in Polish) traditional and other (1950–1). fp Warsaw, 1951 (first seven of eight pieces)

Silesian Triptych, for soprano and orchestra, text traditional, ed. Jan Stanisław Bystron (1951). fp Warsaw, 2 December 1951

Spring and *Autumn,* children's song cycles for mezzo-soprano and chamber orchestra, text (in Polish) by Władysław Domeradzki, Jadwiga Korczakowska, Januszewska and Lucyna Krzemieniecka (1951). fp Warsaw, 1951

Ten Polish Folksongs on Soldiers' Themes, for male choir, text traditional (1951). fp?

Seven Songs, for unison voices and piano, text (in Polish) by Tadeusz Urgacz, Leopold Lewin, Stanisław Wygodzki, Stanisław Ryszard Dobrowolski and Jan Brzechwa (1950–2). fp?

Six Children's Songs, for children's choir and orchestra (1952 arrangement of 1947 voice and piano work). fp Warsaw, 29 April 1954

Six Children's Songs, for mezzo-soprano and orchestra (1952–3 arrangement of 1947 voice and piano work). fp Warsaw, 1954

Silver Window-Pane and *Little Seashell,* children's songs for voice and piano, text (in Polish) by Agnieszka Barto (1953). fp?

Silver Window-Pane and *Little Seashell,* children's songs for mezzo-soprano and chamber orchestra (1953 arrangement of the preceding songs). fp?

Three Songs, for voice (or unison chorus) and piano, text (in Polish) by Stanisław Czachorowski, Aleksander Rymkiewicz and Mieczysław Dołega (1953). fp?

Five Songs to texts by Kazimiera Iłłakowicz, for soprano and piano (1957). fp Katowice, 25 November 1959

Five Songs to texts by Kazimiera Iłłakowicz, for soprano and chamber orchestra (1958 arrangement of the preceding songs). fp Katowice, 12 February 1960

Trois Poèmes d'Henri Michaux, for chorus and orchestra (without strings) (1961–3). fp Zagreb, 9 May 1963

Paroles tissées, for tenor and chamber orchestra, text (in French) by Jean-François Chabrun (1965). fp Aldeburgh, 20 June 1965

Les Espaces du sommeil, for baritone and orchestra, text (in French) by Robert Desnos (1975). fp Berlin, 12 April 1978

The Holly and the Ivy, for unison voices and piano, text (in English) traditional (1985). fp?

Twenty Polish Carols, for soprano, female choir and small orchestra (1984–9 arrangement of 1946 Twenty Carols, with English translations by Charles Bodman Rae). fp London, 5 December 1985 (seventeen carols, in Polish); Edinburgh, 14 December 1990 (complete work, in English)

Tarantella, for baritone and piano, text (in English) by Hilaire Belloc (1990). fp London, 20 May 1990

Chantefleurs et Chantefables, for soprano and small orchestra, text (in French) by Robert Desnos (1991). fp London, 8 August 1991

Ensemble/Chamber/Instrumental

Piano Sonata (1934). fp 1935

Two Studies, for piano (1941). fp Kraków, 26 January 1948 (No. 1); fp?, No. 2

Variations on a Theme of Paganini, for two pianos (1941). fp Warsaw, 1941

Fifty Contrapuntal Studies, for woodwind (1943–4). fp?

Trio, for oboe, clarinet and bassoon (1944–5). fp Kraków, September 1945

Folk Melodies, twelve easy pieces for piano (1945). fp Kraków, 1947

Recitativo e arioso, for violin and piano (1951). fp Kraków, c. 1952

Bucolics, for piano (1952). fp Warsaw, December 1953

Miniature, for two pianos (1953). fp?

Three Pieces for the Young, for piano (1953). fp?

Dance Preludes, for clarinet and piano (1954). fp Warsaw, 15 February 1955

Dance Preludes, for flute, oboe, clarinet, bassoon, horn and string quartet (1959 arrangement of the preceding work). fp Louny, 10 November 1959

String Quartet (1964). fp Stockholm, 12 March 1965

Invention, for piano (1968). fp?

Sacher Variation, for cello (1975). fp Zurich, 2 May 1976

Epitaph, for oboe and piano (1979). fp London, 3 January 1980

Grave, Metamorphoses for cello and piano (1981). fp Warsaw, 22 April 1981

Mini-Overture, for horn, two trumpets, trombone and tuba (1982). fp Lucerne, 11 March 1982

Chain 1, for chamber ensemble (1983). fp London, 4 October 1983

Partita, for violin and piano (1984). fp Saint Paul, Minnesota, 18 January 1985

Tune, fanfare for trumpet (1985). fp?

Fanfare for CUBE (Cambridge University Brass Ensemble), for horn, two trumpets, trombone and tuba (1987). fp Cambridge, 11 June 1987

Slides, for chamber ensemble (1988). fp New York, 1 December 1988

Fanfare for the University of Lancaster, for four horns, three trumpets, three trombones, tuba and side drum (1989). fp Lancaster, 11 October 1989

Subito, for violin and piano (1992). fp Indianapolis, Indiana, September 1994

Andrzej Panufnik

Even more comprehensively than was the case with Lutosławski, Panufnik lost his entire pre-1944 output in the Warsaw Uprising of that year. The only surviving pieces are apparently the Four Underground Resistance Songs composed in 1943–4, which are duly listed below. Apart from undocumented juvenilia, the manuscripts lost included Variations for piano, and Classical Suite for string quartet (both composed c. 1933; the latter was publicly performed at the time in Warsaw); for orchestra, Symphonic Variations (1935–6; performed 1936 in Warsaw), Symphonic Allegro and Symphonic Image (1936), Little Overture (c. 1937; performed that year in Warsaw) and Symphony No. 2 (1941; performed 1944 in Warsaw); and the Psalm for soloist, chorus and orchestra, composed in 1936 as his Diploma work.

In Panufnik's case, there is a further, highly unusual category, consisting of works that were lost in the Uprising but subsequently reconstructed from memory. Details of the three that still exist (Five Polish Peasant Songs, *Tragic Overture* and the Piano Trio) are given below. Symphony No. 1 was also reconstructed and performed in Kraków in 1945, but Panufnik was dissatisfied with the work and subsequently destroyed the score.

Orchestral

Tragic Overture (1942, reconstructed 1945, revised 1955). fp Warsaw, March 1944

Divertimento for Strings, edited and adapted from Six Trios by Felix Janiewicz (1947, revised 1955). fp Kraków, 1948

Lullaby (1947, revised 1955). fp Kraków, 1948

Nocturne (1947, revised 1955). fp Paris, 1948

Sinfonia Rustica (1948, revised 1955). fp Kraków, 1948

Old Polish Suite, based on sixteenth- and seventeenth-century Polish works (1950, revised 1955). fp Warsaw, 1951

Concerto in modo antico, for solo trumpet, two harps, harpsichord and strings, original title: *Koncert Gotycki* ('Gothic Concerto'), based on early Polish works (1951, revised 1955). fp Kraków, 1951

Heroic Overture (1952, revised 1969). fp Helsinki, 27 July 1952

Rhapsody (1956). fp London, 11 January 1957

Sinfonia Elegiaca, includes material from *Symphony of Peace* (1957, revised 1966). fp Houston, Texas, 21 November 1957

Polonia (1959). fp London, 21 August 1959

Autumn Music, for three flutes, three clarinets, percussion, celesta, piano, harp, violas, cellos and contrabasses (1962, revised 1965). fp Paris, 16 January 1968

Landscape, for string orchestra (1962, revised 1965). fp Twickenham, 13 November 1965

Piano Concerto (1962, revised 1970, recomposed 1972; *Intrada* added as new 1st movement 1982). fp Birmingham, 25 January 1962; London, 8 July 1983 (new three-movement version)

Sinfonia Sacra (1963). fp Monte Carlo, 12 August 1964

Two Lyric Pieces for Young Players: 1, for woodwind and brass; 2, for strings (1963). fp Farnham, 13 May 1963

Hommage à Chopin, for flute and small string orchestra (1966 arrangement of 1949 vocal work). fp London, 24 September 1966

Jagiellonian Triptych, for strings, based on early Polish works (1966). fp London, 24 September 1966

Katyń Epitaph (1967, revised 1969). fp New York, 17 November 1968

Violin Concerto, for violin and small string orchestra (1971). fp London, 18 July 1972

Sinfonia Concertante, for solo flute and harp and small string orchestra (1973). fp London, 20 May 1974

Sinfonia di Sfere (1974–5). fp London, 13 April 1976

Sinfonia Mistica (1977). fp Middlesbrough, England, 17 January 1978

Metasinfonia, for solo organ, timpani and strings (1978). fp Manchester, 9 September 1978

Concerto Festivo (1979). fp London, 17 June 1979

Concertino, for timpani, percussion and strings (1979–80). fp London, 24 January 1981

Paean, for large brass ensemble (or eleven brass instruments) (1980). fp London, 16 November 1980

Sinfonia Votiva (1981, revised 1984). fp Boston, Massachusetts, 28 January 1982

A Procession for Peace (1982–3). fp London, 16 July 1983

Arbor Cosmica, twelve evocations for twelve strings (or string orchestra) (1983). fp New York, 14 November 1984

Bassoon Concerto (1985). fp Milwaukee, Wisconsin, 18 May 1986

Symphony No. 9 (*Sinfonia di Speranza*) (1986, revised 1990). fp London, 25 February 1987

Symphony No. 10 (1988, revised 1990). fp Chicago, Illinois, 1 February 1990

Harmony, a poem for chamber orchestra (double woodwind, strings without contrabasses) (1989). fp New York, 15 December 1989

Cello Concerto (1991). fp London, 24 June 1992

Vocal

Five Polish Peasant Songs, for sopranos (or trebles), two flutes, two clarinets and bass clarinet, text (in Polish and Russian) anonymous (1940, reconstructed 1945, revised 1959). fp Kraków, 1945

Four Underground Resistance Songs, for voice (or unison voices) and piano, text (in Polish) by Stanisław Ryszard Dobrowolski (1943–4). fp?

Hommage à Chopin, five vocalises for soprano and piano, originally titled Suita Polska, wordless (1949, revised 1955). fp Paris, 3 October 1949

Symphony of Peace, for chorus and orchestra, text (in Polish) by Jarosław Iwaszkiewicz (1951). fp Warsaw, May 1951. Withdrawn; orchestral material used in 1957 *Sinfonia Elegiaca*

Song to the Virgin Mary, for unaccompanied chorus or six solo voices, text (in Latin) anonymous (1964, revised 1969). fp London, 26 April 1964

Universal Prayer, for soloists (soprano, alto, tenor, bass), chorus, three harps and organ, text (in English) by Alexander Pope (1968–9). fp New York, 24 May 1970

Thames Pageant, cantata for young players and singers, text (in English) by Camilla Jessel (1969). fp Twickenham, 7 February 1970

Invocation for Peace, for trebles, two trumpets and two trombones, text (in English) by Camilla Jessel (1972). fp Southampton, 28 November 1972

Winter Solstice, for soprano and baritone soloists, chorus, three trumpets, three trombones, timpani and glockenspiel, text (in English) by Camilla Jessel (1972). fp Kingston-upon-Thames, 16 December 1972

Love Song, for mezzo-soprano and harp (or piano), text (in English) by Sir Philip Sidney (1976; optional string orchestra part added in 1991). fp London, 1976; London, 28 November 1991 (string orchestra version)

Dreamscape, for mezzo-soprano and piano, wordless (1977). fp London, 12 December, 1977

Prayer to the Virgin of Skempe, for solo voice or unison chorus and organ or instrumental ensemble, text (in Polish) by Jerzy Peterkiewicz (1990). fp complete work with Peterkiewicz poem read in Polish Warsaw, 27 October 1992

Chamber/Instrumental

Piano Trio (1934, reconstructed 1945, revised 1977). fp Warsaw, 1935

Twelve Miniature Studies, for piano, original title: *Circle of Fifths* (1947, Book I revised 1955, Book II revised 1964). fp Kraków, 1948

Quintetto Accademico, for flute, oboe, clarinet, horn and bassoon (1953, revised 1956; score rediscovered 1994). fp?

Reflections, for piano (1968). fp London, 21 April 1972

Triangles, for three flutes and three cellos (1972). fp London, 14 April 1972

String Quartet No. 1 (1976). fp London, 19 October 1976

String Quartet No. 2 (*Messages*) (1980). fp St Asaph's, Wales, 25 September 1980

Pentasonata, for piano (1984). fp Aldeburgh, 23 June 1989

Song to the Virgin Mary, for string sextet (1987 arrangement of vocal work). fp London, 21 February 1988)

String Sextet (*Train of Thoughts*) (1987). fp London, 21 February 1988

String Quartet No. 3 (*Wycinanki,* 'Paper Cuts') (1990). fp London, 15 April 1991

Ballet

The first two scores were specially composed or adapted by the composer for ballet use. The rest are ballets choreographed to existing Panufnik scores (the titles are the same as the original score unless otherwise indicated).

Cain and Abel (reworking of *Sinfonia Sacra* and *Tragic Overture,* together with new material), choreographed by Kenneth MacMillan (1968). fp Berlin, 1968

Miss Julie (reworking of *Nocturne, Rhapsody, Autumn Music* and *Polonia,* together with new material), choreographed by Kenneth MacMillan (1970). fp Stuttgart, 1970

Elegy (to *Sinfonia Elegiaca*): Gerald Arpino, City Center Joffrey Ballet, New York, 1967

Autumn Music: David Drew, BBC TV, London, 1974

The Archaic Moon (to *Rhapsody*): Norman Walker, Houston Ballet, 1978

Adieu (to *Violin Concerto*): David Bintley, Royal Ballet, Covent Garden, London, 1980

Homage to Chopin (to *Hommage à Chopin* and *Mazurek* from *Polonia*): David Bintley, Sadler's Wells Royal Ballet, London, 1980

Polonia: David Bintley, Sadler's Wells Royal Ballet, London, 1980

Dances of the Golden Hall (to *Nocturne*): Martha Graham, Martha Graham Dance Company, New York, 1982

Bogurodzica (to *Sinfonia Sacra*): Gray Veredon, Ballet de l'Opéra de Lyon, 1983

Common Prayer (to *Sinfonia Sacra*): Robert Cohan, Batsheva Dance Company of Israel, 1983

Sinfonia Mistica: Paul Mejia, New York City Ballet, 1987

Vincent van Gogh (to *Sinfonia Sacra*): Raimondo Fornoni, National Ballet of the Netherlands, video production 1987

Sacred Symphony (to *Sinfonia Sacra*): Oliver Hindle, Birmingham Royal Ballet, London, 1991

Sinfonia Concertante: Marie Brolin Tani, Northland Festival, Caithness, Scotland, 1992

Stop It (to Violin Concerto): Krzysztof Pastor, National Ballet of the Netherlands, Amsterdam, 1993

Krzysztof Penderecki

In addition to numerous film scores and sets of incidental music that Penderecki does not regard as part of his enduring *œuvre*, he has withdrawn two works in a more formal manner. These are Two Songs for baritone and piano and an early String Quartet. A Violin Sonata composed in 1953 was also withdrawn at one time, but Penderecki readmitted it to his catalogue in 1990. These three works are included in the appropriate lists below.

Stage Works

The Devils of Loudun (*Die Teufel von Loudun*), opera, libretto by Krzysztof Penderecki after *The Devils of Loudun* by Aldous Huxley, in the dramatization by John Whiting, translated into German by Erich Fried (1968–9). fp Hamburg, 20 June 1969

Paradise Lost, 'sacra rappresentazione', libretto by Christopher Fry after John Milton (1976–8). fp Chicago, Illinois, 29 November 1978

The Black Mask (*Die schwarze Maske*), opera in one act, libretto by Krzysztof Penderecki after the play by Gerhardt Hauptmann (1984–6). fp Salzburg, 15 August 1986

Ubu Rex, opera buffa, libretto by Jerzy Jarocki and Krzysztof Penderecki after the play *Ubu roi* by Alfred Jarry (1990–1). fp Munich, 6 July 1991

Orchestral

Epitafium Artur Malawski in memoriam, for two string orchestras and timpani (1957–8). fp Kraków, September 1959

Emanations, for two string orchestras (1958–9). fp Darmstadt, 7 September 1961

Anaklasis, for strings and percussion (1959–60). fp Donaueschingen, 16 October 1960

Threnody, to the victims of Hiroshima, for fifty-two strings (1960). fp Kraków, September 1961

Fonogrammi, for solo flute and chamber orchestra (1961). fp Venice, 24 April 1961

Polymorphia, for forty-eight strings (1961). fp Hamburg, 6 April 1962

Fluorescences (1961–2). fp Donaueschingen, 21 September 1962

Canon, for strings and two tape recorders (1962). fp Warsaw, 21 September 1962

Three Pieces in Old Style, for strings, based on music from the film *The Saragossa Manuscript* (1963). fp Kraków, 11 June 1988

Sonata for Cello and Orchestra (1964). fp Donaueschingen, 18 October 1964

Capriccio, for oboe and eleven strings (1965). fp Lucerne, 26 August 1965

De natura sonoris No. 1 (1966). fp Royan, 7 April 1966

Cello Concerto No. 1, originally for violino grande (1966–7, revised 1971–2). fp Östersund, 1 July 1967; Edinburgh, 2 September 1972 (revised cello version)

Capriccio, for violin and orchestra (1967). fp Donaueschingen, 22 October 1967

Pittsburgh Overture, for wind band, percussion, harmonium and piano (1967). fp Pittsburgh, Pennsylvania, 30 June 1967

De natura sonoris No. 2 (1970–1). fp New York, 3 December 1971

Actions, for jazz ensemble (1971). fp Donaueschingen, 17 October 1971

Prélude, for wind, percussion, keyboard instruments and contrabasses (1971). fp Amsterdam, 4 July 1971

Partita, for concertante harpsichord, electric guitar, bass guitar, harp, contrabass and orchestra (1971–2, revised 1991). fp Rochester, New York, 11 February 1972; Munich, 5 January 1992 (revised version)

Symphony No. 1 (1972–3). fp Peterborough, 19 July 1973

Intermezzo, for twenty-four strings (1973). fp Zurich, 30 November 1973

The Dream of Jacob (*Als Jakob erwachte …*) (1974). fp Monte Carlo, 14 August 1974

Violin Concerto No. 1 (1976–7, revised 1988). fp Basle, 27 April 1977

Adagietto from *Paradise Lost* (1979). fp Osaka, 8 April 1979

Symphony No. 2 (*Christmas Symphony*) (1979–80). fp New York, 1 May 1980

Cello Concerto No. 2 (1982). fp Berlin, 11 January 1983

Viola Concerto; also cello version by Boris Pergamenshikov (1983). fp Caracas, 21 July 1983; Wuppertal, 15 December 1989 (cello version)

Viola Concerto, for strings, percussion and celesta (1984 rescored version of above work). fp Moscow, 20 October 1985

Passacaglia (1988). fp Lucerne, 20 August 1988; included in Symphony No. 3, fp Munich, 8 December 1995

Adagio – Symphony No. 4 (1989). fp Paris, 26 November 1989

Symphony No. 5 (1991–2). fp Seoul, 14 August 1992

Concerto, for flute and chamber orchestra (1992). fp Lausanne, 11 January 1993

Sinfonietta No. 1, for strings (1992 arrangement of 1993 String Trio). fp Warsaw, 17 February 1992

Entrata, for four horns, three trumpets, three trombones, tuba and timpani (1994). fp Cincinnati, Ohio, 4 November 1994

Sinfonietta No. 2, for clarinet and strings (1994 arrangement of Clarinet Quartet). fp Bad Kissingen, 13 July 1994

Violin Concerto No. 2 (1995). fp Leipzig, 24 June 1995

Vocal

Two Songs, for baritone and piano, text by Leopold Staff (1955–8). Withdrawn

From the Psalms of David, for chorus, strings and percussion, text (in Latin; also Polish, German and English versions) biblical (1958). fp Kraków, September 1959

Strophes, for solo soprano, reciter and ten instruments, text by Menander, Sophocles, Isaiah, Jeremiah and Omar Khayyam (1959). fp Warsaw, 17 September 1959

Dimensions of Time and Silence, for chorus, strings and percussion, wordless (1959–60, revised 1961). fp Kraków, September 1960; Vienna, June 1961 (revised version)

Stabat Mater, for three choirs, text (in Latin) thirteenth-century anonymous, possibly by Jacopone da Todi (1962). fp Warsaw, 27 November 1962

Cantata in honorem Almae Matris Universitatis Iagellonicae, for two choirs and orchestra, text (in Latin) is dedicatory line only (1964). fp Kraków, 10 May 1964

St Luke Passion (*Passio et mors Domini nostri Jesu Christi secundum Lucam*), for soloists (soprano, baritone, bass), speaker, boys' choir, three choirs and orchestra, text (in Latin) biblical (1965–6). fp Münster, 30 March 1966

Dies Irae, oratorio in memory of the victims of Auschwitz, for soloists (soprano, tenor, bass), chorus and orchestra, text assembled by Krzysztof Penderecki from biblical sources, Aeschylus, Władysław Broniewski, Louis Aragon, Tadeusz Różewicz and Paul Valéry, translated into Latin (except Aeschylus) by Tytus Górski (1967). fp Kraków, 14 April 1967 (preliminary performance); Oświecim (Auschwitz), 16 April 1967

Utrenja I, The Entombment of Christ, for soloists (soprano, alto, tenor, bass, basso profondo), two choirs and orchestra, text assembled by Krzysztof Penderecki from Church Slavonic liturgical and biblical sources (1969–70). fp Altenberg, 8 April 1970

Cosmogony, for soloists (soprano, tenor, bass), chorus and orchestra, text assembled by Krzysztof Penderecki from Greek, Latin, Italian, Russian and English sources (1970). fp New York, 24 October 1970

Utrenja II, The Resurrection, for soloists (soprano, alto, tenor, bass, basso profondo), boys' choir, two choirs and orchestra, text assembled by Krzysztof Penderecki from Church Slavonic liturgical and biblical sources (1970–1). fp Münster, 28 May 1971

Ecloga VIII for six male voices (two altos, one tenor, three basses), text by Vergil (1972). fp Edinburgh, 22 August 1972

Canticum Canticorum Salomonis, for sixteen-part chorus, chamber orchestra and two dancers ad lib, text (in Latin) biblical (1970–3). fp Lisbon, 5 June 1973

Magnificat, for solo bass, seven male voices, two choirs, boys' choir and orchestra, text (in Latin) liturgical (1973–4). fp Salzburg, 17 August 1974

Prologue, Visions and Finale from *Paradise Lost*, for six solo voices, large chorus and orchestra (1979). fp Salzburg, 10 August 1979

Te Deum, for soloists (soprano, mezzo-soprano, tenor, bass), two choirs and orchestra, text (in Latin) liturgical, with addition of Polish hymn (1979–80). fp Assisi, 27 September 1980

Lacrimosa, for solo soprano, chorus and orchestra, text (in Latin) liturgical (1980). fp Gdánsk, 16 December 1980

Agnus Dei, for eight-part chorus, text (in Latin) liturgical (1981). fp Warsaw, 30 May 1981

Polish Requiem, for soloists (soprano, alto, tenor, bass), chorus and orchestra, text (in Latin) liturgical, with addition of Polish hymn, incorporates *Lacrimosa* and *Agnus Dei* (1980–4). fp Stuttgart, 28 September 1984

Iże cheruvimi ('Song of Cherubim') for chorus, text traditional Church Slavonic (1986). fp Washington, DC, 27 March 1987

Veni creator, for eight-part chorus, text (in Latin) by Hrabanus Maurus (1987). fp Madrid, 28 April 1987

The Black Mask, two scenes and Finale, for soloists (soprano, mezzo-soprano), chorus and orchestra (1988). fp Poznań, 6 November 1988

Benedicamus Domino, for five-part male chorus, text (in Latin) biblical (1992). fp Lucerne, 18 April 1992

Benedictus, for chorus, text (in Latin) liturgical (1993). Not yet performed at time of publication

Chamber/Instrumental/Electronic

Violin Sonata (1953). fp Houston, Texas, 7 January 1990

Three Miniatures, for clarinet and piano (1956). fp?

String Quartet (1956–7). Withdrawn

Miniatures, for violin and piano (1959). fp Kraków, June 1960

String Quartet No. 1 (1960). fp Cincinnati, Ohio, 11 May 1962

Psalmus 1961, electronic music (1961). fp Stockholm, 10 April 1961

Brigade of Death, electronic music for a radio play (1963). fp Warsaw, 20 January 1964

Capriccio for Siegfried Palm, for cello solo (1968). fp Bremen, 4 May 1968

Capriccio, for tuba solo (1980). fp Kraków, 20 June 1980

Cadenza, for viola solo; also violin version by Christiane Edinger (1984). fp Lusławice, 10 September 1984; Warsaw, 28 October 1986 (violin version)

Per Slava, for cello solo (1985–6). fp?

Prelude, for clarinet solo (1987). fp?

Der unterbrochene Gedanke, for string quartet (1988). fp Frankfurt, 4 February 1988

String Trio (1990–1). fp Kraków, 8 December 1990 (2nd movement); Metz, 15 November 1991 (complete work)

Clarinet Quartet (1993). fp Lübeck, 13 August 1993

Ballet

The following works were choreographed to Penderecki scores (the titles are the same as the original score unless otherwise indicated).

Metropolis (to Symphony No. 1): Fay Werner, City Theatre, Münster, 1975

Traum des Galilei (to Symphony No. 1): William Forsythe, Stuttgart Ballet, Stuttgart, 1978

Magnificat (see **Vocal**): Tanzstudio of the Folkwang-Hochschule, Essen, 1981

Capriccio (to *Capriccio for Siegfried Palm*): Munich State Opera, 1992

Prometheus (to music from Intermezzo for twenty-four strings, Adagietto from *Paradise Lost*, *The Dream of Jacob*, *Dies Irae* and *Utrenja*): Jurek Makarowski, Dortmund, 1992

Credo (to music from *Canticum Canticorum Salomonis*, Sonata for Cello and Orchestra, *Threnody* and *De natura sonoris*): Mai Murdmaa, Estonian Theatre, Tallinn, 1994

Further Reading

For a general view of the subject from its beginnings to 1965, when the book was published, *Polish Music,* edited by Stefan Jarociński (Warsaw, PWN – Polish Scientific Publishers, in English) remains an excellent source if you can find it. For readers of German, the article 'Gesichter der Postmoderne' by Andrzej Chłopecki in *Musiktexte* No. 44, April 1992 (referred to in Chapter 6) contains thought-provoking and highly intelligent discussion of Górecki, Penderecki and others. The American conductor Richard Dufallo's collection of conversations, *Trackings,* contrives in its freewheeling way to draw a wealth of illuminating comment from both Lutosławski and Penderecki (as well as twenty-four other composers).

Henryk Górecki

The articles by Adrian Thomas revived interest in Górecki in Western circles, and are the best source of information about him. The Marek/Drew piece also contains vital background matter, and the more recent Drew article is characteristically incisive in the distinction it draws between the integrity of the composer and the excesses of some of his exploiters.

Drew, D. 'Górecki's Millions', in *The London Review of Books,* October 1994

Davies, L. 'Górecki' in B. Morton and P. Collins (eds.) *Contemporary Composers* (Chicago and London, St James Press, 1992)

Marek, T. and Drew, D. 'Górecki in Interview (1968) – and Twenty Years After', in *Tempo* No. 168, March 1988

Mellers, W. 'Round and about Górecki's Symphony No. 3', in *Tempo* No. 168, March 1988

Pociej, B. 'Górecki', in S. Sadie (ed.) *The New Grove Dictionary of Music and Musicians* (London, Macmillan, 1980)

Thomas, A. 'A Pole Apart: the Music of Górecki since 1965', in *Contact* No. 28, Autumn 1984

Thomas, A. 'The Music of Henryk Mikołaj Górecki: the First Decade', in *Contact* No. 27, Autumn 1983

Witold Lutosławski

Of the writings cited, I have found Stucky and Varga the most consistently helpful on their quite different scales. Stucky, himself a gifted composer, provides the best musical discussion of Lutosławski, and his bibliography, though allegedly 'selective', is astoundingly thorough: if Stucky has not read it, it has not been written. Rae seems to know his Poland, and his comprehensive book has the advantage of being in a position to consider the composer's entire output; biographically it contains much invaluable information, but on music his knowledge impresses more than his understanding. Varga's little set of probing conversations achieves an importance out of all proportion to its size. Much of the biographical information contained in Chapter 2 draws on these three sources and on Richard Dufallo's and Tadeusz Kaczyński's interviews with the composer.

Dufallo, R. (ed.) 'Witold Lutosławski', in *Trackings (Composers Speak with Richard Dufallo)* (New York and Oxford, Oxford University Press, 1989)

Kaczyński, T. *Conversations with Witold Lutosławski* (London, Chester Music, English edition 1984)

Nordwall, O. (ed.) *Lutosławski* (Stockholm, Hansen, in English, 1968)

Rae, C. B. *The Music of Lutosławski* (London and Boston, Faber and Faber, 1994)

Stucky, S. *Lutosławski and His Music* (Cambridge, Cambridge University Press, 1981)

Varga, B. A. (ed.) *Lutosławski Profile*, consisting of conversations with the composer (London, Chester Music, English edition 1974)

Andrzej Panufnik

Composing Myself, Panufnik's autobiography, is more about life than works, and evokes the situation of an artist living in a totalitarian Communist state with horrifying vividness; but for someone who hated talking about his music Panufnik writes remarkably well about that too. His *Impulse and Design* booklet lays bare the conceptual foundation of several of his scores with a concise text and some pretty diagrams.

Osborne, N. 'Panufnik at 70', *Tempo* No. 150, September 1984

Panufnik, A. *Impulse and Design in My Music* (London, Boosey & Hawkes, 1974)

Panufnik, A. *Composing Myself* (London, Methuen, 1987)

Potter, T. 'All My Children: a Portrait of Andrzej Panufnik', in *The Musical Times* Vol. cxxxii No. 1778, April 1991

Truscott, H. 'The Achievement of Andrzej Panufnik', in *Tempo* No. 163, December 1987

Krzysztof Penderecki

Wolfram Schwinger, who has himself played a considerable role in Penderecki's career, presents a sensitive and well-organized account of the man and his work, and the late William Mann's translation is exemplary.

Dufallo, R. (ed.) 'Krzysztof Penderecki', in *Trackings (Composers Speak with Richard Dufallo)* (New York and Oxford, Oxford University Press, 1989)

Pociej, B. 'Penderecki', in S. Sadie (ed.) *The New Grove Dictionary of Music and Musicians* (London, Macmillan, 1980)

Schwinger, W. *Krzysztof Penderecki: his Life and Work* (London, Schott; English edition of *Penderecki: Leben und Werk* including new material 1989; further expanded German edition published by Schott Mainz, 1995)

Selective Discography

In this list of recommended recordings, which covers
four composers' work, the principles of inclusion are
necessarily varied. Many works by Lutosławski and
Penderecki have been recorded several times, both
under the composers' own direction and by other
conductors; questions of choice are also complicated by
the existence of several anthology discs and collections.
(Works should be looked for both under individual
headings, such as 'vocal' and 'orchestral', and in the
'collections' list at the head of each composer's entry.)
Panufnik recorded several works himself, but there are
few duplications from other hands. In Górecki's case
there are few duplications at all (except of the Third
Symphony) and no recordings by the composer. This
list includes a representative selection of each
composer's work with the following qualifications: the
composer's own interpretative voice always deserves a
hearing; where there is a version of a key work
conducted by the composer, an alternative is normally
also included if there is a good one; when several
versions of major works have varying merits, all those
that seem to me worthy of choice are included; LPs
and cassettes are only included either when there is no
other version of a work available, or when the
recording in question has historic value, and certain
CDs are also included on the latter ground – under
these headings the world première of Górecki's Third
Symphony and old versions of some concertos played
by their dedicatees are included.

Henryk Górecki

Collections

Epitafium
Scontri
Genesis 2
Refrain
Old Polish Music
National Philharmonic Choir of Warsaw, Polish Radio
National Symphony Orchestra of Katowice conducted
by Jan Krenz, Warsaw National Philharmonic
Orchestra conducted by Andrzej Markowski
POLSKIE NAGRANIA MUZA XL 0391;
OLYMPIA OCD 385

Old Polish Music
Beatus Vir
Totus Tuus
Nikita Storojev (bass), Prague Philharmonic Choir,
Czech Philharmonic Orchestra conducted by John
Nelson
ARGO 436 835–2

Three Pieces in Old Style
Amen
Symphony No. 3
Warsaw National Philharmonic Chamber Orchestra
conducted by Karol Teutsch, Poznań Boys' Choir
conducted by Jerzy Kurczewski, Stefania Woytowicz
(soprano) and Polish Radio National Symphony
Orchestra of Katowice conducted by Jerzy Katlewicz
POLSKIE NAGRANIA PNCD 215;
OLYMPIA OCD 313

Harpsichord Concerto
Good Night
Kleines Requiem für eine Polka
Elzbieta Chojnacka (harpsichord) with London
Sinfonietta conducted by Markus Stenz, Dawn
Upshaw (soprano), various soloists conducted by
David Zinman
ELEKTRA NONESUCH 7559 79362

Vocal

Symphony No. 2
Beatus Vir
Emese Soós (soprano), Tamás Altorjay (baritone),
Bartók Chorus, Fricsay Symphonic Orchestra
conducted by Tamás Pál
STRADIVARIUS STR 33324

Euntes Ibant et Flebant
Amen
Broad Waters
Miserere
My Vistula, Grey Vistula
Chicaco Symphony Chorus and Chicago Lyric Opera
Chorus conducted by John Nelson, Lira Chamber
Chorus conducted by Lucy Ding
ELEKTRA NONESUCH 9 79348–2

Symphony No. 3
Stefania Woytowicz (soprano), Southwest German
Radio Symphony Orchestra conducted by Ernest Bour
(live recording, world première, Royan, 1977)
BELART 437 964–2

Symphony No. 3
Dawn Upshaw (soprano), London Sinfonietta
conducted by David Zinman
ELEKTRA NONESUCH 9 79282–2

Symphony No. 3
Joanna Kozłowska (soprano), Warsaw Philharmonic
Orchestra conducted by Kazimierz Kord
PHILIPS 442 411–2

Orchestral

Symphony No. 1
Three Pieces in Old Style
Choros I
Kraków Philharmonic Orchestra conducted by Roland
Bader
KOCH SCHWANN 3–1041–2

Harpsichord Concerto (piano version)
Three Pieces in Old Style
Anna Górecka (piano), Amadeus Chamber Orchestra
conducted by Agnieska Duczmal; with string orchestra
works by Kilar, Szymanowski/Duczmal, Bacewicz and
Shostakovich/Barshai
CONIFER CDCF 246

Chamber/Instrumental/Large Ensemble

Four Preludes
Piano Sonata
David Arden; with piano works by Pärt and
Ustvolskaya
KOCH INTERNATIONAL 3-7301-2

Toccata
Maria Nosowska and Barbara Halska (pianos); with
piano and two-piano works by Chopin, Pankiewicz,
Brzeziński, Różycki, Kamieński, Lutosławski,
Twardowski and Borkowski
OLYMPIA OCD 394

Sonata for two violins
Genesis 1
Already it is Dusk
Quasi una Fantasia
Silesian String Quartet, Marek Moś (conductor)
OLYMPIA OCD 375

Recitatives and Ariosos – Lerchenmusik
Already it is Dusk
London Sinfonietta Soloists, Kronos Quartet
ELEKTRA NONESUCH 9 79257–2

Already it is Dusk
Quasi una Fantasia
Kronos Quartet (same performance of *Already it is
Dusk* as in previous listing)
ELEKTRA NONESUCH 9 79319–2

Recitatives and Ariosos – Lerchenmusik
Kleines Requiem für eine Polka
Schönberg Ensemble conducted by Reinbert de Leeuw
PHILIPS 442533–2

Witold Lutosławski

Collections

Lacrimosa
Symphony No. 1
Concerto for Orchestra
Funeral Music
Stefania Woytowicz (soprano), Silesian Philharmonic
Choir, Polish Radio National Symphony Orchestra of
Katowice conducted by Witold Lutosławski and by Jan
Krenz, Warsaw National Philharmonic Orchestra
conducted by Witold Rowicki
POLSKIE NAGRANIA PNCD 040

Two Studies
Variations on a Theme of Paganini
Five Songs
String Quartet
Epitaph
Grave (cello and piano arrangement)
Partita
Marek Drewnowski (piano), Jacek and Maciej
Łukaszczyk (two pianos), Halina Łukomska (soprano)
with Warsaw National Symphony Orchestra
conducted by Andrzej Markowski, LaSalle String
Quartet, Heinz Holliger (oboe) and Szábolcs Esztényi
(piano), Roman Jabłoński (cello) and Szábolcs Esztényi
(piano), Konstanty Andrzej Kulka (violin) and
Eugeniusz Knapik (piano)
POLSKIE NAGRANIA PNCD 045

Symphony No. 1
Les Espaces du sommeil
Chain 3
Symphony No. 4
Warsaw National Philharmonic Orchestra conducted
by Witold Lutosławski, François Le Roux (baritone)
(live recording, Warsaw Autumn Festival, 1993)
KOS WJ 001

Postlude No. 1
Paroles tissées
Livre pour orchestre
Cello Concerto
Polish Radio National Symphony Orchestra of
Katowice conducted by Jan Krenz, Louis Devos (tenor)
and Warsaw National Philharmonic Orchestra
conducted by Witold Lutosławski, Warsaw National
Philharmonic Orchestra conducted by Jan Krenz,
Roman Jabłoński (cello) and Polish Radio National
Symphony Orchestra of Katowice conducted by
Witold Lutosławski
POLSKIE NAGRANIA PNCD 042

Jeux vénitiens
Trois Poèmes d'Henri Michaux
Symphony No. 2
Warsaw National Philharmonic Orchestra conducted
by Witold Rowicki and Witold Lutosławski, Polish
Radio Choir of Kraków conducted by Witold
Lutosławski and Polish Radio National Symphony
Orchestra of Katowice conducted by Jan Krenz
POLSKIE NAGRANIA PNCD 041

Les Espaces du sommeil
Symphony No. 3
Dietrich Fischer-Dieskau (baritone), Berlin
Philharmonic Orchestra conducted by Witold
Lutosławski
PHILIPS 416 387–2

Les Espaces du sommeil
Symphony No. 3
Symphony No. 4
John Shirley Quirk (baritone), Los Angeles
Philharmonic conducted by Esa-Pekka Salonen
SONY CLASSICAL SK 66280

Orchestral

Symphonic Variations
Symphony No. 1
Funeral Music
Symphony No. 2
Polish National Radio Symphony Orchestra of
Katowice conducted by Witold Lutosławski
EMI MATRIX CDM 5 65076 2

Concerto for Orchestra
Jeux vénitiens
Livre pour orchestre
Mi-parti
Polish National Radio Symphony Orchestra of
Katowice conducted by Witold Lutosławski
EMI MATRIX CDM 5 65305 2

Concerto for Orchestra
Symphony No. 3
Chicago Symphony Orchestra conducted by Daniel
Barenboim
ERATO 4509–91711–2

Dance Preludes (orchestral version)
Janet Hilton (clarinet), Scottish National Orchestra
conducted by Matthias Bamert; with clarinet concertos
by Copland and Nielsen
CHANDOS CHAN 8618

Cello Concerto
Mstislav Rostropovich, Orchestre de Paris conducted
by Witold Lutosławski; with *Tout un monde lointain …*
by Dutilleux
EMI CDC 7 49304 2

Preludes and Fugue
Mi-parti
Novelette
Warsaw National Chamber Orchestra and Polish Radio
National Symphony Orchestra of Katowice conducted
by Witold Lutosławski, Junge Deutsche Philharmonie
conducted by Heinz Holliger
POLSKIE NAGRANIA PNCD 043

Novelette
Chain 3
Piano Concerto
Krystian Zimerman (piano), BBC Symphony
Orchestra conducted by Witold Lutosławski
DEUTSCHE GRAMMOPHON 431 664-2

Double Concerto
Heinz and Ursula Holliger (oboe and harp), Cincinnati
Symphony Orchestra conducted by Michael Gielen;
with Strauss Oboe Concerto
VOX CUM LAUDE MCD 10006

Symphony No. 3
Chain 1
Chain 2
Chain 3
Polish Radio National Symphony Orchestra of
Katowice conducted by Antoni Wit and Witold
Lutosławski, Junge Deutsche Philharmonie conducted
by Heinz Holliger, Krzysztof Jakowicz (violin) and
Warsaw National Philharmonic Orchestra conducted
by Kazimierz Kord
POLSKIE NAGRANIA PNCD 044

Chain 2
Isabelle van Keulen (violin), Philharmonia Orchestra
conducted by Heinrich Schiff
KOCH SCHWANN 3-1523-2

Chain 2
Partita
Anne-Sophie Mutter (violin), Phillip Moll (piano
obbligato in Partita), BBC Symphony Orchestra
conducted by Witold Lutosławski
DEUTSCHE GRAMMOPHON 423 696-2

Ensemble/Chamber/Instrumental

Variations on a Theme of Paganini
Martha Argerich and Nelson Freire (two pianos); with
two-piano works by Rachmaninov and Ravel
PHILIPS 411 034–2

Variations on a Theme of Paganini
Maria Nosowska and Barbara Halska (two pianos);
with piano and two-piano works by Chopin,
Pankiewicz, Brzeziński, Różycki, Kamieński, Górecki,
Twardowski, and Borkowski
OLYMPIA OCD 394

String Quartet
Kronos Quartet
ELEKTRA NONESUCH 7559–79255–2

Mini-Overture
Meridian Arts Ensemble; with brass quintet works by
Hindemith, Harut'unyan, Taxin, Jan Bach and Etler
CHANNEL CLASSICS CCS 2191

Andrzej Panufnik

Collections

Universal Prayer
Metasinfonia
April Cantelo (soprano), Helen Watts (alto), John
Mitchinson (tenor), Roger Stalman (bass), Louis
Halsey Singers and instrumental soloists conducted by
Leopold Stokowski, Jennifer Bate (organ), Kurt-Hans
Goedicke (timpani), London Symphony Orchestra
conducted by Andrzej Panufnik
UNICORN-KANCHANA DKP 9049 (LP)

Vocal

Song to the Virgin Mary
Camerata Silesia conducted by Anna Szostak; with
choral works by Palestrina, Zieleński, Verdi and
Palester
MUSICON MCD 007

Thames Pageant
Invocation for Peace
John Amis (commentator), King's House School
Choir, Thames Youth Ensemble conducted by Michael
Stuckey
UNICORN-KANCHANA UNS 264 (LP)

Dreamscape
Meriel and Peter Dickinson (mezzo-soprano and
piano); with works for voice and piano by Harvey,
Dickinson, Crosse, and Lutyens
UNICORN-KANCHANA DKP(CD)9093

Orchestral

Tragic Overture
Nocturne
Sinfonia Rustica
Heroic Overture
Autumn Music
London Symphony Orchestra conducted by Jascha
Horenstein, Monte Carlo Opera Orchestra conducted
by Andrzej Panufnik
UNICORN-KANCHANA UKCD 2016

Rhapsody
Louisville Orchestra conducted by Robert Whitney;
with Orchestral Fantasy by Blacher
LOUISVILLE LS 671 (LP)

Sinfonia Elegiaca
Louisville Orchestra conducted by Robert Whitney;
with Symphony No. 2 by Orrego-Salas
LOUISVILLE LS 624 (LP)

Piano Concerto
Symphony No. 9
Ewa Pobłocka (piano), London Symphony Orchestra
conducted by Andrzej Panufnik
CONIFER CD CF 206

Landscape
Sinfonia Sacra
Katyń Epitaph
Concerto Festivo
Concertino
Kurt-Hans Goedicke and Michael Frye (timpani and
percussion), London Symphony Orchestra conducted
by Andrzej Panufnik, Monte Carlo Opera Orchestra
conducted by Andrzej Panufnik
UNICORN-KANCHANA UKCD 2020

Sinfonia Sacra
Arbor Cosmica
Concertgebouw Orchestra of Amsterdam and New
York Chamber Symphony conducted by Andrzej
Panufnik
ELEKTRA NONESUCH 9 79228-2

Hommage à Chopin (orchestral version)
Violin Concerto
Bassoon Concerto
Karen Jones (flute), Krzysztof Smietana (violin),
Robert Thompson (bassoon), London Musici
conducted by Mark Stephenson
CONIFER CDCF 182

Hommage à Chopin (orchestral version)
Radik Suleimanov (flute), Leningrad Philharmonic
Chamber Orchestra conducted by Gennady
Rozhdestvensky; with orchestral works by Janáček,
Webern, Bach/Schoenberg, Ives and Shostakovich
MELODIYA C10 1149–50 (LP)

Violin Concerto
Sinfonia Concertante
Yehudi Menuhin (violin), Aurèle Nicolet (flute), Osian
Ellis (harp), Menuhin Festival Orchestra conducted by
Andrzej Panufnik
EMI EMD 5525 (LP)

Violin Concerto
Arbor Cosmica
Robert Kabara (violin), Sinfonietta Cracovia
conducted by Wojciech Michniewski
DUX 0254

Sinfonia Concertante
Concertino
Harmony
Karen Jones (flute), Rachel Masters (harp), Graham
Cole (timpani), Richard Benjafield (percussion),
London Musici conducted by Mark Stephenson
CONIFER CDCF 217

Sinfonia di Sfere
Sinfonia Mistica
London Symphony Orchestra conducted by David
Atherton
DECCA HEAD 22 (LP)

Paean
The Band and Fanfare Trumpeters of the Royal
Military School of Music conducted by Lt. Col. G.
Evans; in collection 'Military Music Through the Ages'
BANDLEADER MILITARY BND 61003 (cassette)

Sinfonia Votiva
Boston Symphony Orchestra conducted by Seiji
Ozawa; with Sessions Concerto for Orchestra
HYPERION CDA66050

Sinfonia Votiva
BBC Symphony Orchestra conducted by Andrzej
Panufnik; with Symphonies Nos. 3 and 4 by
Szymanowski (live recording, Promenade Concerts,
London, 1983)
BBCRD 9124

Cello Concerto
Mstislav Rostropovich, London Symphony Orchestra
conducted by Hugh Wolff
NMC D010S

Chamber

String Quartets Nos. 1–3
String Sextet
Song to the Virgin Mary (sextet version)
Chilingirian String Quartet, Roger Chase (viola),
Stephen Orton (cello)
CONIFER CDCF 218

Krzysztof Penderecki

Collections

Violin Sonata
Lacrimosa
Ize cheruvimi
Sinfonietta No. 1 for Strings
Concerto for flute and chamber orchestra
Benedicamus Domino
Clarinet Quartet
Grigori Zhislin (violin) and Vladimir Viardo (piano),
Warsaw National Philharmonic Choir, Sinfonia
Varsovia conducted by Henryk Wojnarowski and
Krzysztof Penderecki, Jean-Pierre Rampal (flute),
Sharon Kam (clarinet), Christoph Poppen (violin),
Kim Kashkashian (viola) and Boris Pergamenshikov
(cello) (live recording, Warsaw, 1993)
SONY CLASSICAL SK 66284

From the Psalms of David
Dimensions of Time and Silence
St Luke Passion
Threnody
Polymorphia
String Quartet No. 1
Warsaw National Philharmonic Choir and Orchestra
conducted by Andrzej Markowski, Stefania Woytowicz
(soprano), Andrzej Hiolski (baritone), Bernard Ładysz
(bass), Leszek Herdegen (speaker), Kraków
Philharmonic Boys' and Mixed Choirs and Orchestra
conducted by Henryk Czyż, Warsaw National
Philharmonic Orchestra conducted by Witold
Rowicki, Kraków Philharmonic Orchestra conducted
by Henryk Czyż, LaSalle Quartet
POLSKIE NAGRANIA PNCD 017 (2 CDs)

From the Psalms of David
Anaklasis
Sonata for Cello and Orchestra
Fluorescences
Stabat Mater
Warsaw National Philharmonic Choir and Percussion
Group and Warsaw National Philharmonic Orchestra,
Siegfried Palm (cello) and Poznań Philharmonic
Orchestra, Warsaw National Philharmonic Choir,
conducted by Andrzej Markowski
WERGO WER 60020 (LP)

Canticum Canticorum Salomonis
Anaklasis
Threnody
Fonogrammi
De natura sonoris No. 1
Capriccio for violin and orchestra
De natura sonoris No. 2
The Dream of Jacob
Kraków Philharmonic Chorus, Wanda Wiłkomirska
(violin), London Symphony Orchestra, Polish Radio
National Symphony Orchestra of Katowice conducted
by Krzysztof Penderecki
EMI MATRIX CDM 5 65077 2

Strophes
Three Pieces in Old Style
Capriccio for oboe and eleven strings
Intermezzo
Viola Concerto
Olga Szwajgier (soprano), Mariusz Pędziałek (oboe),
Tabea Zimmermann (viola), Amadeus Chamber
Orchestra conducted by Agnieszka Duczmal
WERGO WER 60172–50

Vocal

From the Psalms of David
Stabat Mater and *Psalms* (from *St Luke Passion*)
Sicut locutus est (from *Magnificat*)
Agnus Dei (from *Polish Requiem*)
Veni creator spiritus
Iże cheruvimi
Warsaw National Philharmonic Chorus and
instrumental soloists of Warsaw National Philharmonic
conducted by Krzysztof Penderecki
WERGO WER 6261-2

St Luke Passion
Sigune von Osten (soprano), Stephen Roberts
(baritone), Kurt Rydl (bass), Edward Lubaszenko
(speaker), Kraków Boys' Choir, Warsaw National
Philharmonic Chorus, Polish Radio National
Symphony Orchestra of Katowice conducted by
Krzysztof Penderecki
ARGO 430 328–2

Dies Irae
Polish Requiem
Stefania Woytowicz (soprano), Wiesław Ochman
(tenor), Bernard Ładysz (bass), Kraków Philharmonic
Choir and Orchestra conducted by Henryk Czyż,
Jadwiga Gadulanka (soprano), Jadwiga Rappé (alto),
Henryk Grychnik (tenor), Carlo Zardo (bass), Polish
Radio and Television Choir of Kraków, Kraków
Philharmonic Choir, Polish Radio National Symphony
Orchestra of Katowice conducted by Antoni Wit
POLSKIE NAGRANIA PNCD 021 (2CDs)

Utrenja
Delfina Ambroziak and Stefania Woytowicz
(sopranos), Krystyna Szczepańska (mezzo-soprano),
Kazimierz Pustelak (tenor), Włodzimierz Denysenko,
Bernard Ładysz, Boris Carmeli and Peter Lagger
(basses), Pioneer Choir, Warsaw National
Philharmonic Choir and Orchestra conducted by
Andrzej Markowski
POLSKIE NAGRANIA PNCD 018

Polish Requiem
Ingrid Haubold (soprano), Grażyna Winogrodska
(mezzo-soprano), Zachos Terzakis (tenor), Malcolm
Smith (bass), North German Radio Choir, Bavarian
Radio Choir, North German Radio Symphony
Orchestra conducted by Krzysztof Penderecki (live
recording, Jesuit Church, Lucerne, 1989)
DEUTSCHE GRAMMOPHON 429 720–2 (2 CDs)

Orchestral

Emanations
Fonogrammi
Canon
Cello Concerto No. 1
Capriccio for violin and orchestra
De natura sonoris No. 2
Partita for harpsichord and orchestra
Siegfried Palm (cello), Wanda Wiłkomirska (violin),
Felicja Blumental (harpsichord), Polish Radio National
Symphony Orchestra of Katowice conducted by
Krzysztof Penderecki
EMI SLS 850 (2LPs)

The Dream of Jacob
Adagietto (from *Paradise Lost*)
Cello Concerto No. 2
Viola Concerto
Ivan Monighetti (cello), Stefan Kamasa (viola), Polish
Radio National Symphony Orchestra of Katowice
conducted by Antoni Wit
POLSKIE NAGRANIA PNCD 020

Violin Concerto No. 1
Isaac Stern (violin), Minnesota Orchestra conducted by
Stanislaw Skrowaczewski
CBS MASTERWORKS 76739 (LP)

Violin Concerto No. 1
Symphony No. 2
Konstanty Andrzej Kulka (violin) and Polish Radio
National Symphony Orchestra of Katowice conducted
by Krzysztof Penderecki and Jacek Kasprzyk
POLSKIE NAGRANIA PNCD 019

Violin Concerto No. 1
Cello Concerto No. 2
Christiane Edinger (violin), Boris Pergamenshikov
(cello), Bamberg Symphony Orchestra conducted by
Krzysztof Penderecki
ORFEO C 285 931 A

Symphony No. 2
Adagio – Symphony No. 4
North German Radio Symphony Orchestra conducted
by Krzysztof Penderecki
WERGO WER 6270–2

Chamber/Instrumental

Violin Sonata
Three Miniatures
Miniatures
String Quartets Nos. 1 and 2
Capriccio for Siegfried Palm
Cadenza
Per Slava
Prelude
Der unterbrochene Gedanke
Konstanty Andrzej Kulka (violin) and Waldemar
Malicki (piano), Aleksander Romański (clarinet) and
Szábolc Esztényi (piano), Silesian String Quartet, Ivan
Monighetti (cello), Artur Paciorkiewicz (viola)
WERGO WER 6258–2

String Quartets Nos. 1 and 2
Prelude
Der unterbrochene Gedanke
String Trio
Clarinet Quartet
Tale Quartet, Martin Fröst (clarinet)
BIS CD–652

Index

Page numbers in italics refer to picture captions

Photographic Acknowledgements

Associated Press, London: 93–5
Boosey and Hawkes, London: 197,
201; photograph by Selwyn
Green 186–7; photograph by
Jean Guyaux 165; photograph
by Adrian Thomas 182t
Camera Press: 159
Chester Music, London: 67, 68,
72l, 80, 84t, 108, 114–15
Malcolm Crowthers: 98, 167, 188,
191, 192–3, back cover
Hulton Deutsch Collection: 10t+b,
11t+b, 13b, 22–3, 26, 29, 30–1,
32, 35, 36–7, 42, 43, 70–1, 76–7,
82, 84b, 88–9, 116, 125r+b,
128–9, 134–5, 136, 141, 142–3,
157, 169, 170, 172–3, 179b, 181,
182b, 185
Iwaszkiewicz Archives, photograph
by Camilla Jessel: 78
Tadeusz Kaczynski-Andrzej
Panufnik, I Jego Muzyka: 101

Lebrecht Collection: 13t+r, 15, 47,
72b, 74, 96, 99, 178, 179t;
photograph by Betty Freeman
97
Lyric Opera of Chiacago: 155
Moeck Verlag, Celle: 202
National Museum of Warsaw:
124l+r
Observer: 190
Panufnik Archives, photograph by
Camilla Jessel: cover, 17, 19l+r,
20, 24, 33, 39, 41, 45, 53, 56, 58,
60–1, 63, 64; Herald
Photography 117, 119
Ronald Grant Archive: 125tl
Royal College of Music: 13cl
B. Schott's Söhne, Mainz: 195, 204
Wolfram Schwinger: 131, 137, 140,
163; photograph by Niggi
Brauning 153; photograph by
Stanislaw Chmiel 151;
photograph by Salzburger
Festspiele 146l; photograph by
B. Friedrich 160–1; photograph
by Hannes Kilian 2, 131;
photograph by Anne Kirchbach
146r; photograph by Werner
Schloske 145; photograph by
Sabine Toepffer 148–9
Warner Classics: 189
Warsaw Autumn: 50–1, 65, 86,
90–1, 154–5, 171, 175t+b, 176